HALF BAKED HARVEST
Quick & Cozy

HALF BAKED HARVEST
Quick & Cozy

TIEGHAN GERARD

CLARKSON POTTER/PUBLISHERS

NEW YORK

To my supportive HBH community,
I created this book with you all in
mind. It's filled with the recipes we
all need on busy days. I tried to keep
them simple but still super yummy—
and, of course, they all have a special
Tieghan touch that makes them just
a little bit more delicious. I hope they
make you feel cozy!

contents

introduction

Hello again!

I can't believe I am sharing another cookbook with you. It's crazy to me that we already have three books together under our belts—and now, here we are with the latest. I might be a bit too attached, but the recipes ahead of you are my absolute favorite yet. Let me tell you why . . .

I feel like I wrote my first cookbook, *Half Baked Harvest*, forever ago. I was only twenty-two years old, and I have grown so much since then! Those recipes reflected that time in my life: they were a bit more detailed, maybe somewhat time intensive, and I just wrote in a different way than I do today. *Super Simple* focused heavily on Instant Pot, slow cooker, and skillet dinners. The idea was obvious and winning—I know many of you love it the most! And most recently was *Every Day*. I love that book: it shares balanced recipes that reflect my everyday lifestyle. It has a lot of color and a wonderful variety of flavors.

And now, here we are with *Quick & Cozy*! I feel the most confident about this book so far, and let me tell you, I AM SO FREAKING EXCITED!!! If you all knew what it took to get these ideas from my head to the book you hold in your hands now, you would understand even more, but I really put everything I have into these pages. And just like the title promises, the recipes are quick and cozy—and totally delicious!

But let me tell you what else *Quick & Cozy* means to me. Well, the quick part is pretty obvious—most of the recipes in this book are doable in under 45 minutes, and lots of them can be prepared in under 30. And the cozy part . . . yes, there are warm stews and hearty food in this book, but cozy is not just for wintertime. Really for me, cozy is about memories of growing up with my then-six brothers and our dad getting dinner on the table late at night. Summers back in Cleveland enjoying Dad's fresh-grown basil, falls spent craving Mom's pot roast, winter days hanging out with my Nonnie while she made chili, and spring vacations with the family cooking up the best burgers. A big part of the way I create is relying on my memories, especially the ones surrounding food and scents, and turning them into amazing meals to share with you. This book is full of memories I've made with my mom and dad, my brothers, my sister, my Nonnie, my many cousins, and the people we've added to our family over the years. So many great experiences have turned into so many delicious recipes.

In the usual HBH way, I've organized this book by types of meals and ingredients. And, as always, I've included tags for the easiest browsing experience for you. Throughout these pages, you'll find meals that are 10 ingredients or less, 30 minutes or less, one-pan, gluten-free, and vegetarian. The stories at the top of each recipe page share a special memory, a cooking tip, or a serving suggestion. The idea is that everyone can cook from this book!

ingredients

There is nothing fussy or fancy about these recipes. I have aimed to use the simplest ingredients. I'll tell you about my standard items below; you probably already have them at home! And there are some special things I've picked up over time that have really added so much flavor to my cooking that I want to introduce them to you, if you don't already know them.

I prefer to cook and bake with **fine pink Himalayan salt**. Himalayan salt boasts all eighty-four essential trace elements that our bodies need to function properly. It is also known to promote stable blood sugar levels, reduce muscle cramping, facilitate an optimal pH in your cells, and more. But I am definitely not a doctor, so that's about all I have! I love salt and I love the way this salt tastes, so why not use something that's also working hard for me?

I also use a lot of **flaky salt** to finish dishes. It is so pretty and adds the best little bursts of flavor right to the top of your food! I exclusively use **salted butter**, just like my mom taught me, but a lot of people don't prefer this. Keep in mind all my recipes are developed with salted butter, so if you use unsalted, you might need to add more salt to your dish! Also, always **large eggs** when baking.

Okay, and if we are talking key ingredients, I do have a few flavorful tricks up my sleeve. They keep things quick and cozy—these give a lot of payoff for just a little

addition. You will notice I love **gochujang chili paste**, for its tangy, spicy, warm flavor and use it in many recipes—not just in those that have Korean-inspired flavors. (For example, it's hidden in my favorite meatballs on page 210!) I also love **Calabrian chiles** for their unique flavor, plus they come smashed into a paste and packed in oil, which makes them easy to mix into pretty much any recipe. And you can't beat their spicy flavor: it's not overpowering, but adds a good kick! They're super easy to find online. I have been a fan of oil-packed **sun-dried tomatoes** forever (the Whole Foods 365 brand is my favorite) because honestly, I just find them delicious. Their concentrated flavor, texture, color . . . I eat them from the jar, like olives! I even think they can replace ingredients like bacon or prosciutto if you're looking for a vegetarian swap. It's not the same, but they do add something. And I also make great use of the oil they're soaking in! **Thai red curry paste** adds a great kick of complex Thai herbs and spices without added sugar or funky ingredients. You can just as easily use it as a marinade as you can a base for a quick dressing mixed with oil. A couple of tablespoons goes a long way! I also use a lot of Mexican **salsa verde**. The brand I use, Sabor Mexicano, has hand-roasted tomatillos, jalapeños, cilantro, water, and sea salt—that's it—but it has THE BEST flavor! I would totally make this at home, but they did a better job. It's not too spicy and has a good smokiness. I love the charred pieces of peppers in the sauce, too. Oh, and I do love **ketchup**—but that's just a little fun fact. (There isn't much ketchup in my recipes, but while we're at it, I use Rao's or Primal Kitchen, which has no sugar added!)

Now it's time to turn the page and have fun finding all the recipes you want to cook, bake, and, fingers crossed, enjoy! I encourage you to use lots of sticky notes and mark your personal changes to each recipe so you can make them the way YOU love them next time. Those are the signs of a great cookbook! And don't forget the marinara sauce stains, too.

I can't wait to see what you cook up! Whether you're here for the fourth time or the first time, thank you for coming along. I promise you, this is the best Half Baked Harvest book yet!

five quick tips to get cozy

- Buy a rotisserie chicken from the store, shred it up, and keep it in your fridge. Use it in soups, enchiladas, quesadillas, and even in salad. Or for extra effort, roast your own on Sunday, then use that throughout the week.

- If pizza is on the menu for the week ahead, make your dough over the weekend. You can let pizza dough sit for a few days; it will develop more flavor. Or keep some in the freezer!

- Use a cookie scoop to make your meatballs—it's so easy and much less messy!

- When you're working with chicken, use heavy kitchen shears instead of a knife to cut it into bite-size pieces. And if you work directly over a sheet pan or bowl: you won't even have to dirty the cutting board!

- Save your Parmesan rinds in a zip-top bag in the freezer! Any time you feel the urge, throw one into your soup—they add amazing flavor. And a cool tip I learned from Nadia Caterina Munno, The Pasta Queen, herself: you can and should eat the cooked rind. It's the most flavorful part of the cheese!

breakfast

maple bacon pancakes
with bourbon maple syrup

PREP TIME 20 minutes · **COOK TIME** 30 minutes · **TOTAL TIME** 50 minutes, plus resting time · **SERVES** 6

I have a deep, deep love of pancakes. When I first started cooking, I would make banana pancakes for my mom what seemed like every other day. She loved them so much, and she still does—I will still make them for her for dinner on a random night when nothing else is coming out of my kitchen. In these pancakes, though, I removed the banana and added crispy bacon, which is even better. These almost feel like a maple bacon doughnut. My mom, the pancake princess, has given these two thumbs up on multiple occasions. When I have the time, I like to make a quick, bourbon-infused maple syrup, too. If you don't like to cook with alcohol, leave it out or replace the bourbon with a tablespoon of vanilla extract.

Pancakes

3 tablespoons salted butter, plus more for cooking and serving

2 cups white whole-wheat flour

1½ teaspoons baking powder

1½ teaspoons baking soda

½ teaspoon fine pink Himalayan salt

2 cups buttermilk

2 large eggs

1 tablespoon maple syrup

2 teaspoons pure vanilla extract

1 (16-ounce) package sliced bacon, cooked

Bourbon Maple Syrup

1 cup maple syrup

3 tablespoons bourbon (optional)

1 cinnamon stick

1. Make the pancakes. Melt the butter in a small saucepan over medium heat and cook until it just begins to brown, about 3 minutes. Transfer the butter to a small bowl; it will continue browning slightly. Set aside to cool but not harden.

2. In a large bowl, stir together the flour, baking powder, baking soda, and salt. Add the buttermilk, eggs, maple syrup, vanilla, and brown butter. Whisk to combine well; some lumps in the batter are okay. Cover with a clean kitchen towel and let rest for about 10 minutes.

3. Meanwhile, make the syrup. In the same saucepan used for melting the butter, combine the maple syrup, bourbon (if using), and the cinnamon stick. Set over low heat and cook until fragrant and lightly bubbling, 8 to 10 minutes. Remove the pan from the heat and discard the cinnamon stick.

4. In a large skillet or griddle over medium heat, and working in batches, lay down a strip or two of bacon, then pour about ¼ cup of the batter over the bacon (it might not cover the bacon completely). Cook until bubbles appear on the surface, about 2 minutes, then use a spatula to gently flip the pancake. Cook on the second side until golden, 1 to 2 minutes more. Reserving several slices of bacon, repeat with the bacon and the remaining batter.

5. Crumble the reserved bacon strips and sprinkle over the pancakes. Serve topped with butter and the bourbon maple syrup.

spicy eggs in purgatory
with chile-sesame butter

PREP TIME 15 minutes · COOK TIME 30 minutes · TOTAL TIME 45 minutes · SERVES 4 to 6

When you have guests over for breakfast, make this dish. The sauce is simple and delicious, with a combination of Calabrian chile paste, roasted red peppers, and fresh herbs. I love to top the whole thing with crumbled feta cheese and my homemade garlic tahini. The tahini is unexpected, but it is usually the sauce that everyone loves the most! Plus, it pairs well with these eggs.

1 tablespoon extra-virgin olive oil

3 garlic cloves, smashed

1 (28-ounce) can crushed fire-roasted tomatoes

1 (16-ounce) jar roasted sliced red peppers, drained

1 to 2 tablespoons crushed Calabrian chile peppers

Fine pink Himalayan salt

4 to 6 large eggs

4 ounces feta cheese, crumbled

1 cup fresh herbs, such as dill, cilantro, parsley, and/or basil, chopped

Chile-Sesame Butter (recipe follows)

Garlic Tahini

1/2 cup tahini

1 tablespoon fresh lemon juice

1 garlic clove, finely chopped or grated

1 teaspoon fine pink Himalayan salt

Sliced crusty bread, for serving (optional)

1. Heat the olive oil in a large skillet over medium heat. When the oil is shimmering, add the garlic and cook until fragrant, 1 minute. Add the tomatoes, roasted red peppers, Calabrian chiles, and salt. Reduce the heat to medium-low and cook, stirring occasionally, until the mixture begins to thicken, about 15 minutes.

2. Meanwhile, make the garlic tahini. In a small bowl, combine the tahini, 1/4 cup of ice water, the lemon juice, garlic, and salt. Stir until fully mixed. If it seems too thick, add more water, by the tablespoon, to reach a thin, flowing consistency.

3. Using the back of a spoon, make 4 to 6 divots in the sauce, then carefully crack one egg into each divot. Cover and cook until the eggs are cooked to your liking, 5 to 6 minutes for runnier yolks or 8 to 10 minutes to cook through.

4. To serve, crumble the feta over the eggs. Top with the herbs, then dollops of chile-sesame butter and garlic tahini. Serve with plenty of crusty bread for scooping, as desired.

chile-sesame butter
—————— MAKES ABOUT 1/4 CUP ——————

3 tablespoons salted butter

2 teaspoons Aleppo pepper

1/2 teaspoon sweet paprika

1 tablespoon sesame seeds

Fine pink Himalayan salt

In a small saucepan, combine the butter, Aleppo pepper, and paprika. Cook over low heat until the butter is melted, 2 to 3 minutes. Stir in the sesame seeds, remove from the heat, and season with salt. Use immediately or let cool and store in an airtight container in the refrigerator for up to 3 months. To use, spread or melt as desired.

chocolate chip pumpkin muffins

PREP TIME 20 minutes · **COOK TIME** 20 minutes · **TOTAL TIME** 40 minutes · **MAKES** 16 or 17 muffins

These muffins—sooo much to love here! They're simply spiced, lightly sweetened, extra pumpkin-y, and stuffed with chocolate chips. Plus, they're a one-bowl wonder. You can't beat these for a quick breakfast or an afternoon treat! What makes these muffins so special is the pumpkin butter: not only does it add a rich flavor, but it also yields the softest, sweetest pumpkin muffins. My little sister, Asher, loves to warm these up before eating them to get the chocolate all melty again. If it's a chilly day, she'll pair them with a mug of hot cocoa—a perfect combination!

½ cup coconut oil, melted

½ cup maple syrup or honey

2 teaspoons pure vanilla extract

2 large eggs, at room temperature

1 cup pumpkin butter

1 cup canned pumpkin puree

2 cups all-purpose or white whole-wheat flour, plus more as needed

1½ teaspoons baking soda

½ teaspoon baking powder

1½ teaspoon ground cinnamon

¼ teaspoon ground cloves

1 teaspoon fine pink Himalayan salt

1 cup semisweet chocolate chips

1. Preheat the oven to 350°F. Using two 12-cup muffin tins, line 16 cups with paper liners.

2. In a large bowl, combine the coconut oil, maple syrup, vanilla, eggs, pumpkin butter, and pumpkin puree. Whisk until smooth and well combined. Add the flour, baking soda, baking powder, cinnamon, cloves, and salt and mix until just combined. Fold in the chocolate chips.

3. Divide the batter among the muffin cups, filling each three-quarters of the way. If you have more batter, grab another paper liner and fill it up.

4. Bake for 18 to 22 minutes, until the muffin tops are just set and a tester inserted into the centers comes out clean. Enjoy warm, ideally! Store at room temperature in an airtight container for up to 5 days.

chai-spice swirl quick bread

PREP TIME 25 minutes · **COOK TIME** 1 hour · **TOTAL TIME** 1 hour 25 minutes, plus cooling time · **SERVES** 8

I love the fall more than any other season. It's such a special time, filled with excitement for the holidays, pumpkin spice lattes, crisp air, and, of course, plenty of baking. I start making this quick bread in September, before I break out the pumpkin in October. It's such a cozy, warm, and delicious loaf, and the chai spices smell amazing as it bakes. My tip for you: Bake two of these loaves at the same time, then grab some cute food packaging to wrap one up and use as a host/hostess gift or as a surprise treat for a friend.

Chai-Spice Ginger Crunch

3 tablespoons salted butter, melted, plus more for serving

1/2 cup packed light brown sugar

1/4 cup granulated sugar

2 tablespoons all-purpose flour

2 tablespoons chopped crystallized ginger

2 tablespoons ground cinnamon

1 teaspoon ground cardamom

1/2 teaspoon freshly grated nutmeg

1/2 teaspoon ground allspice

1/2 teaspoon ground cloves

1/4 teaspoon ground ginger

1/4 teaspoon freshly ground black pepper

Quick Bread

1/3 cup melted coconut oil, plus more for greasing

2/3 cup milk of your choice

1/2 cup full-fat plain Greek yogurt

1/2 cup maple syrup or honey

1 large egg

1 tablespoon pure vanilla extract

2 cups all-purpose flour

1 teaspoon baking soda

1/2 teaspoon fine pink Himalayan salt

1. Preheat the oven to 350°F. Grease a 9 x 5-inch loaf pan with coconut oil.

2. Make the chai-spice ginger crunch. In a medium bowl, combine the melted butter, both sugars, the flour, crystallized ginger, cinnamon, cardamom, nutmeg, allspice, cloves, ground ginger, and pepper. Stir to mix and set aside.

3. Make the quick bread. In a large bowl, stir together the milk, yogurt, maple syrup, coconut oil, egg, and vanilla until combined. Add the flour, baking soda, and salt and stir just until the flour disappears.

4. Spoon half of the batter into the prepared pan and use a flexible spatula to smooth the top. Add half of the chai-spice ginger crunch, scattering it evenly. Spoon the remaining batter on top, smooth into an even layer, and then cover with an even coating of the remaining crunch.

5. Bake until a tester inserted into the center comes out clean, 55 to 60 minutes. Remove the pan from the oven and place on a wire rack to cool for 10 minutes. Loosen from the sides of the pan with a knife, invert onto the rack, and then carefully turn over so the crunchy top is facing up. Enjoy warm or at room temperature, slathered with salted butter.

grated egg avocado toast

PREP TIME 10 minutes · **TOTAL TIME** 10 minutes · **MAKES** 4 to 6 toasts

If I'm not making pancakes or French toast for breakfast, I'm definitely making eggs. And eggs are perfect with a great piece of avocado toast—don't you agree? Most often, I am frying my eggs in a skillet, cooking them over easy, but when I am crunched for time in the morning, I grab a couple hard-boiled eggs from the fridge (I love to keep them on hand), then grate them on a box grater—just like you would cheese. It's a fun and different way to switch up the usual. Spicy mayo makes the toast even more delicious! A little honey and sea salt on top, too. So yummy!

$^1/_2$ cup mayonnaise

1 teaspoon hot sauce
(I like Frank's RedHot)

1 teaspoon smoked paprika

$^1/_4$ teaspoon chili powder

$^1/_4$ teaspoon cayenne pepper,
plus more as needed

Fine pink Himalayan salt

1 large avocado

Juice of 1 lemon

4 to 6 slices sourdough
bread, toasted

4 to 6 large hard-boiled eggs

For Serving

Hot honey

Flaky sea salt

Chopped fresh herbs, such
as basil, mint, or parsley

1. In a small bowl, combine the mayo, hot sauce, paprika, chili powder, and cayenne. Taste and add pink salt as needed. Scoop out the avocado into a separate small bowl. Squeeze in the lemon juice and mash to mix well.

2. Spread one side of each piece of toast with the mayo mixture, then add the avocado. Using a cheese grater, grate an egg directly onto each slice of bread.

3. Drizzle each toast with hot honey and sprinkle with flaky salt. Garnish with herbs and serve.

mini corn soufflé omelets

PREP TIME 15 minutes · **COOK TIME** 15 minutes · **TOTAL TIME** 30 minutes · **MAKES** 16 mini omelets

My mom adores corn soufflé, and she requests it every year for Thanksgiving. But why can't we have our favorite holiday foods on regular days? I started making these one summer, and now they are a breakfast staple for us. The key is the whipped egg—they are what gives you that light and fluffy soufflé texture. Be very gentle when working with the whipped whites, as they can deflate easily. Patience is your friend with this recipe! Sprinkle these minis with sea salt and thyme—and serving them with a little drizzle of honey or a dusting of Parmesan would be delicious, too!

Softened butter, for greasing

2 cups corn kernels, fresh (from 4 ears) or thawed if frozen

6 large eggs, separated

1/3 cup heavy cream

2 green onions, chopped

1 tablespoon fresh thyme leaves, plus more for serving

1 teaspoon smoked paprika

1/2 teaspoon cayenne pepper

Fine pink Himalayan salt and freshly ground black pepper

3/4 teaspoon cream of tartar

1 cup shredded Gruyère cheese

1 cup fresh baby spinach, chopped

Flaky sea salt, for serving

1. Preheat the oven to 350°F. Grease two 12-cup muffin tins. Divide the corn evenly among 16 of the cups.

2. In a medium bowl, whisk the egg yolks with the cream, green onions, thyme, paprika, cayenne, and a pinch each of salt and pepper.

3. In a separate medium bowl, using an electric mixer, beat the egg whites with a pinch of salt until foamy, about 30 seconds, then add the cream of tartar. Continue to mix on medium speed until glossy peaks form, 2 to 3 minutes. Using a spatula, gently fold the egg whites into the yolk mixture just to combine. Gently fold in the Gruyère and spinach.

4. Divide the batter among the muffin cups, filling each three-quarters of the way.

5. Bake for 15 to 20 minutes, until deeply golden and puffed. Run a knife around the edge of the muffin tin cups to release and remove the omelets. Serve topped with fresh thyme and flaky salt. Store refrigerated in an airtight container for up to 5 days.

note: Make a double batch and freeze them for an easy weekday breakfast. After baking and cooling, arrange the mini omelets in a single layer in a freezer storage bag and seal–they'll keep for up to 3 months. Thaw them in the microwave and enjoy!

sun-dried tomato pesto egg sandwich

PREP TIME 15 minutes · **COOK TIME** 10 minutes · **TOTAL TIME** 25 minutes · **MAKES** 2 to 4 sandwiches

Of all the egg recipes I'm sharing here, I think I love this one most. I like to pan-fry my eggs in butter and cook them over easy, just like my dad does. Then I layer the hot eggs on toasted focaccia with sun-dried tomato pesto and a fresh mix of arugula and herbs. The spicy chile butter is extra, but it also makes everything extra delicious! Just cook the eggs however you like them and, I promise, you will love this sandwich. I like to use Trader Joe's focaccia, but if you have a hard time finding focaccia in your grocery store, ciabatta is equally great!

1 loaf (10- to 12-ounce) focaccia bread, halved crosswise

Chile-Sesame Butter (page 21)

¼ cup Sun-Dried Tomato Pesto (page 183) or store-bought sun-dried tomato pesto

2 ounces goat cheese, crumbled

1 avocado, sliced

1 teaspoon lemon zest plus 1 tablespoon fresh lemon juice

2 cups baby arugula

Fine pink Himalayan salt

1 tablespoon salted butter

4 large eggs

1 tablespoon chopped fresh dill

1. Heat the broiler to high.

2. Arrange the focaccia cut-side up on a baking sheet. Broil until toasted, about 2 minutes, then remove from the broiler.

3. Pour the chile-sesame butter over the cut side of both pieces of focaccia, dividing it evenly. Spread the tomato pesto over the bottom piece and then sprinkle the goat cheese over the pesto. Add the avocado slices, using a fork to mash them into the pesto and cheese. Add the lemon zest and juice, then the arugula. Season with salt.

4. Melt the butter in a skillet over medium-high heat and cook the eggs to your liking. Slide them over the arugula. Sprinkle with the dill and finish with the top piece of bread. Cut into portions and serve hot.

cheesy ham & broccoli egg bake

PREP TIME 20 minutes · **COOK TIME** 50 minutes · **TOTAL TIME** 1 hour 10 minutes · **SERVES** 6 to 8

If you read my website, you probably know that my mom was always the baker when I was growing up. She didn't cook much, but she always handled holiday dinners and big brunches. Christmas-morning breakfast is her specialty. When my brothers and I were young, she would make a waffle strata, kind of like a savory bread pudding, with Eggos, cheese, and a simple egg batter like what you would use for French toast. She asked me to re-create the strata without using frozen waffles, and this is it! Instead, I love to use flaky croissants, then I add melty Gruyère and top it with ham or prosciutto before baking, which gets nice and crispy. This bake is now my mom's favorite Christmas-morning meal. You can even assemble it the night before, then pop it in the oven—it's great to entertain with!

3 tablespoons cold salted butter, thinly sliced, plus more at room temperature for greasing

2 cups whole milk

6 large eggs

1 tablespoon Dijon mustard

2 teaspoons dried thyme

1 teaspoon onion powder

$1/2$ teaspoon cayenne pepper

Fine pink Himalayan salt and freshly ground black pepper

20 to 24 mini croissants (I like Whole Foods brand), about 20 ounces total

2 cups broccoli florets, chopped

1 cup shredded Gruyère cheese

3 ounces thinly sliced deli ham or prosciutto, torn

1 cup shredded fontina cheese

Fresh thyme leaves, for serving

1. Preheat the oven to 350°F. Grease a 10- or 12-inch round baking dish.

2. In a large bowl, whisk together the milk, eggs, mustard, dried thyme, onion powder, and cayenne, and season with salt and pepper. Working in batches, submerge the croissants into the egg mixture, allowing them to soak for about 1 minute per side. Arrange the croissants in the prepared baking dish.

3. Add the broccoli and Gruyère to the remaining egg mixture in the bowl. Stir to combine, then pour it over the croissants. Arrange the ham over the top, then evenly scatter with the fontina.

4. Cover the baking dish with aluminum foil and bake until the cheese is melting and the egg mixture begins to set, about 30 minutes. Remove the foil, scatter the butter slices over the top, and continue baking, uncovered, until the croissants are golden and the cheese is completely melted, 15 to 20 minutes more.

5. Sprinkle with fresh thyme and serve warm, family style.

cinnamon waffles

PREP TIME 15 minutes · COOK TIME 40 minutes · TOTAL TIME 55 minutes, plus resting time ·
MAKES 12 regular or 24 mini waffles

As a kid, I ate *a lot* of frozen waffles—my brothers and I particularly loved the cinnamon toast flavor. We would toast them, then slather them with way too much butter. I re-created those waffles with this recipe, and I can say for sure that homemade is much better than the store-bought. Find a small waffle iron if you can, to better replicate the classic inspiration. The butter melts into the nooks and crannies, and, of course, the cinnamon syrup adds to all the deliciousness. Do *not* skip it!

Salted butter, for greasing and serving

1¾ cups whole milk or milk of your choice

½ cup full-fat plain Greek yogurt

2 large eggs

1 tablespoon honey

1 tablespoon pure vanilla extract

2 cups white whole-wheat flour

1 tablespoon baking powder

1 teaspoon ground cinnamon

½ teaspoon fine pink Himalayan salt

Cinnamon Syrup

½ cup honey

⅓ cup maple syrup

3 cinnamon sticks

1. Grease a waffle iron with butter and preheat.

2. In a large bowl, whisk together the milk, yogurt, eggs, honey, and vanilla. Add the flour, baking powder, cinnamon, and salt. Mix until just combined. It's okay if there are small lumps. Let the batter rest for about 10 minutes.

3. **Meanwhile, make the cinnamon syrup.** In a small saucepan, combine the honey, maple syrup, and cinnamon sticks. Cook over low heat, stirring often, until the flavors are melded, about 5 minutes. Do not let the mixture boil. Remove the pan from the heat and remove the cinnamon sticks.

4. Cook the waffles according to the manufacturer's directions, brushing the waffle iron lightly with butter between each batch. Serve the waffles with butter and cinnamon syrup.

pesto egg & avocado bacon wraps

PREP TIME 20 minutes · COOK TIME 10 minutes · TOTAL TIME 30 minutes · MAKES 4 wraps

The first time I had Caesar salad was at Champs, a restaurant in Cleveland, Ohio, which has since closed. I was in sixth grade and out to lunch with my Nonnie. When I ordered the Caesar salad, Nonnie looked at me with the funniest face. She said, "You do know that salad has raw eggs in it, don't you?" I didn't think it was a big deal so I enjoyed my chicken Caesar . . . that is, until afterward! Related to the egg or not, it was my first and, thankfully, only experience with food poisoning. After that, I avoided Caesar salad for the longest time, but now I love it! I started making my own dressing, which changed the game for me. This dressing is perfect in this yummy breakfast wrap—so good with the cheesy eggs and creamy avocado!

Caesar Dressing

$^1/_2$ cup mayonnaise

3 tablespoons
extra-virgin olive oil

3 tablespoons fresh lemon juice

2 teaspoons Dijon mustard

2 teaspoons
Worcestershire sauce

1 to 2 garlic cloves, finely
chopped or grated

$^1/_3$ cup freshly grated
Parmesan cheese

Fine pink Himalayan salt and
freshly ground black pepper

Wraps

6 large eggs

Fine pink Himalayan salt

2 tablespoons salted butter

$^1/_2$ cup shredded pepper Jack
cheese or crumbled blue cheese

2 cups baby spinach

2 cups sprouts or microgreens

2 avocados, diced

$^1/_4$ cup fresh basil, torn

4 large flour tortillas

$^1/_2$ cup basil pesto

6 to 8 slices bacon,
cooked and crumbled

1. Make the Caesar dressing. In a medium bowl, combine the mayo, olive oil, lemon juice, mustard, Worcestershire, and garlic. Stir in the Parmesan. Taste and add salt and pepper as needed.

2. Make the wraps. In a medium bowl, beat together the eggs and salt. Melt the butter in a medium skillet over medium heat. Pour in the eggs and cook without stirring just until they begin to set on the bottom, about 1 minute. Sprinkle with the cheese. Using a spatula, lift up the edges of the eggs and let the uncooked egg run underneath. Scatter the spinach over the top, and continue to cook until the eggs are set and the spinach is slightly wilted, 1 minute more. Remove the skillet from the heat.

3. Meanwhile, in a medium bowl, combine the sprouts, avocado, and basil. Add half of the Caesar dressing and gently stir to coat.

4. Working one at a time, microwave a tortilla for 15 to 20 seconds to soften. Spread with a layer of pesto, then carefully add a one-quarter portion of the spinach-topped eggs followed by crumbled bacon. Top with the sprouts mixture and gently roll as for a wrap, placing seam-side down on a serving plate. Repeat with remaining ingredients and serve with remaining Caesar dressing for dipping.

salsa verde breakfast tacos

PREP TIME 10 minutes · **COOK TIME** 20 minutes · **TOTAL TIME** 30 minutes · **MAKES** 4 tacos

A few of my friends live in Austin, and they are constantly talking about how good breakfast tacos are in their city. The last time I was in town, I finally got to go out for a breakfast run to see what all the hype was about, and I have to say, the tacos did not disappoint! I adore salsa verde, so I ordered all the tacos with salsa verde. Austin breakfast tacos are SO GOOD. I immediately started making this recipe on weekends back home. These tacos are really simple—my secret is crisping the cheese in a skillet, then adding the eggs. The eggs cook up in the oil from the cheese as the cheese gets crispy and crunchy. Such a wonderful way to cook your eggs!

$^1\!/_2$ cup shredded Colby Jack cheese

$^1\!/_2$ cup shredded jalapeño Jack cheese

4 small corn tortillas, warmed (see Note)

4 large eggs

$^3\!/_4$ cup salsa verde

1 avocado, lightly mashed

Fine pink Himalayan salt

$^1\!/_2$ cup chopped fresh cilantro

2 green onions, thinly sliced

Chile-Sesame Butter (page 21), for serving

1. In a medium bowl, combine both cheeses. Stack the warmed tortillas together and cover them with a clean towel to keep warm.

2. Heat a medium nonstick skillet over medium-low heat. Working in batches, add one-quarter of the cheese mixture in a circle, about the size of a tortilla. When the cheese starts to melt, about 30 seconds, crack an egg into the center of the circle. Cook until the edges are beginning to set, about 1 minute. Add a spoonful of salsa verde and continue to cook until the egg reaches your desired doneness and the cheese is crispy, 3 to 4 minutes more. Repeat with the remaining ingredients.

3. Meanwhile, divide the avocado evenly among the tortillas, spreading it to the edges. Season with salt.

4. Carefully place the cooked egg and cheese on top of the avocado. Finish with the cilantro, green onion, and chile-sesame butter. Serve with any remaining salsa verde alongside.

note: I like to very carefully warm tortillas directly over an open flame, watching closely and turning once or twice with heatproof tongs for a few seconds per side, just until they're hot and soft with a little bit of char. If you don't have a gas stove, you can do this in a dry skillet or in the microwave.

butterflake biscuits
with salted honey butter

PREP TIME 35 minutes · **COOK TIME** 25 minutes · **TOTAL TIME** 1 hour · **MAKES** 12 biscuits

These biscuits have become a staple for me. I make them a lot on the weekends, or sometimes even to serve with dinner. They are quick and easy to pull together, and they're great when you feel like baking bread but don't have time to mess around with anything yeasted. There are two secrets to making these: first, instead of breaking out your food processor to chop the cold butter, we are going to grate it on a box grater as if it were cheese. That grated butter creates the absolute flakiest biscuit—I use this method a lot! Second, when you're cutting your biscuits, be sure to make one straight cut. Don't wiggle the knife around, otherwise you'll risk losing some of the flaky layers, which you definitely want! Serve the biscuits warm with plenty of salty honey butter—perfection.

Biscuits

2½ cups all-purpose flour, plus more as needed

1 tablespoon baking powder

1 teaspoon fine pink Himalayan salt

½ cup (1 stick) very cold salted butter, grated with large holes of a box grater, plus 2 cold tablespoons, sliced

1 cup cold buttermilk, plus more for brushing

2 teaspoons honey

Honey Butter

4 tablespoons (½ stick) salted butter, at room temperature

3 tablespoons honey, plus more for serving

Flaky sea salt

1. Make the biscuits. Preheat the oven to 425°F. Grease a 10- or 12-inch cast-iron skillet.

2. In a large bowl, stir together the flour, baking powder, and salt. Add the grated butter and use your hands to mix it into the flour until a dough forms. Pour in the buttermilk and add the honey. Continue mixing until just combined.

3. Turn the dough out onto a lightly floured surface and pat into a 1-inch-thick rectangle. Fold one edge into the center, then the other, like a letter. Turn the dough 180 degrees, use your hands to flatten it into a 1-inch-thick rectangle again, and repeat the folding. Turn the dough 180 degrees again and flatten it into a ¾-inch-thick rectangle. Use a sharp knife to cut the dough into 8 square biscuits. Arrange the biscuits in the prepared skillet. Brush the tops with buttermilk, then scatter the sliced butter all around.

4. Bake the biscuits until golden brown, 20 to 22 minutes.

5. Meanwhile, make the honey butter. In a small bowl, stir together the butter, honey, and a pinch of flaky salt.

6. Remove the biscuits from the oven, split, and immediately spread with the honey butter. Enjoy with extra honey and flaky salt.

apps, snacks & cocktails

the brothers' game day snack mix

PREP TIME 15 minutes · COOK TIME 30 minutes · TOTAL TIME 45 minutes · SERVES 10 to 12

My brothers are BIG fantasy football guys—and they request this mix for Sunday game days all fall long. According to them, it is totally irresistible, and they're not wrong! I love making homemade buffalo sauce (see page 176 if you'd like to make your own), and then I toss it with pretzels, Cheez-Its, and Chex cereal. Add some Parmesan and garlic and bake it all up. It gets gobbled up quickly, so you'll probably want to make an extra-big batch!

6 tablespoons (¾ stick) salted butter, melted

2 to 4 tablespoons hot sauce (I like Frank's RedHot)

1 tablespoon Homemade Seasoned Salt (page 56) or store-bought seasoned salt

2 teaspoons smoked paprika

2 teaspoons dried parsley

1 teaspoon dried dill

3 cups salted mini pretzel twists

3 cups mixed Cheez-Its and/or Goldfish crackers

2 cups Rice Chex cereal

1 cup mini saltine crackers

½ cup freshly grated Parmesan cheese

1 garlic clove, finely chopped or grated

1. Preheat the oven to 300°F.

2. In a large bowl, stir together the butter, hot sauce, seasoned salt, paprika, parsley, and dill. Add the pretzels, cheese crackers, cereal, and saltines and toss very well to coat evenly. Add the Parmesan and garlic and toss, toss, toss again.

3. Transfer the mixture to a shallow roasting pan and spread evenly. Bake, tossing once or twice, until lightly toasted and fragrant, about 30 minutes. Transfer to a large bowl to serve. Once cooled, it can be stored at room temperature in an airtight container for up to 1 week—if there's any left over!

cheesy roasted shallot bread

PREP TIME 10 minutes · **COOK TIME** 35 minutes · **TOTAL TIME** 45 minutes · **SERVES** 8

My brother Malachi loves garlic bread. So does my oldest brother, Creighton. You know what? So does my whole family. It's delicious, so I am sure you understand. The only thing I can think of that's better than garlic bread is shallot bread. I think shallots are underrated and underused. I love them! And no shocker here: If you roast shallots with oil and herbs, they become even more delicious. So here we do that, then mash the shallots with butter and spread it all over a piece of ciabatta, add cheese, and bake. It's so wonderful!

4 small shallots, halved lengthwise

4 garlic cloves

1/4 cup extra-virgin olive oil

4 sprigs fresh thyme

Crushed red pepper flakes or Korean chile flakes

4 tablespoons (1/2 stick) salted butter, at room temperature

1 loaf French or ciabatta bread, halved lengthwise

1 tablespoon dried oregano

1 cup shredded mozzarella cheese

1/2 cup shredded Gouda cheese

Fresh herbs, for serving

1. Preheat the oven to 400°F.

2. Place the shallots and garlic in a small baking dish. Add the olive oil and scatter the thyme and red pepper flakes over the oil. Bake until the shallots and garlic are deeply golden and very soft, about 20 minutes. Remove from the oven and leave the oven set to 400°F.

3. Transfer the shallots and garlic to a cutting board, reserving the oil in the baking dish, and let cool slightly. Discard the stems from the thyme. Mash or finely chop the shallots and garlic into a paste and add to the oil in the baking dish. Add the butter and stir to mix well.

4. Spread the shallot-butter paste over the cut sides of the bread. Sprinkle the oregano on top, then the mozzarella and Gouda. Arrange the bread on a baking sheet and bake until the cheese is melted and bubbling, about 15 minutes. Garnish with fresh herbs and serve immediately.

sour cream & onion dill pickle dip

PREP TIME 10 minutes · **TOTAL TIME** 10 minutes · **SERVES 8**

I used to think sour cream and onion chips sounded absolutely awful. How could that combo be good? My mom never served us sour cream, and she claimed to hate onions. But then one of my younger brothers, Red—we call him "the snackster"—started eating sour cream and onion chips. He claims they're the best of the best, flavor-wise. These days, I really can't argue with the flavor combination—it's a good one, and it's even better when you add dill pickles. I make my dip with Greek yogurt and sour cream, which I think is the perfect combo. Plus, the yogurt makes the dip high in protein and even creamier in texture.

1 cup full-fat plain Greek yogurt

³/₄ cup sour cream

¹/₂ cup finely chopped dill pickles

2 tablespoons chopped fresh chives

2 tablespoons dried onion flakes

2 tablespoons dried parsley

1 tablespoon pickle brine

1 garlic clove, finely chopped or grated

2 teaspoons dried dill

Fine pink Himalayan salt and freshly ground black pepper

For Serving

Extra-virgin olive oil

Potato chips

Toasted crusty bread or bagels

Cucumber slices

1. In a medium bowl, combine the yogurt, sour cream, pickles, chives, onion flakes, parsley, pickle brine, garlic, and dill. Stir well to combine. Season with salt and pepper as needed.

2. Drizzle olive oil over the top, then serve with potato chips, toasted bread, bagels, and/or cucumber slices.

crispy, salty sweet potato skin chips

PREP TIME 15 minutes · **COOK TIME** 25 minutes · **TOTAL TIME** 40 minutes · **SERVES** 4

To put it simply, these chips are a delight. I started making them when I took over cooking Thanksgiving dinner. Of course, I make my mom's sweet potato casserole—I like to bake my sweet potatoes whole, then easily peel away the skins. I used to discard the skins, but one year I decided to save them and make chips! At first, I fried them, but now I love to bake them with olive oil and whatever herbs I have on hand, usually sage and/or thyme. But even if you don't have any herbs, these chips are still so delicious with oil and salt. They are perfectly crunchy and, just like any good potato chip, totally addicting.

6 medium sweet potatoes

$1/3$ cup extra-virgin olive oil

1 cup fresh mixed herbs, such as sage, rosemary, and/or thyme, chopped

Flaky sea salt

Tahini Caesar Dressing (page 82) or store-bought Caesar dressing, for serving

Ketchup, for serving

1. Preheat the oven to 450°F. Line a baking sheet with parchment paper.

2. Trim the ends of the potatoes to create two flat sides. Using a knife, carefully slice the potato skins into long strips from end to end, leaving about $1/4$-inch flesh attached. Reserve the sweet potato centers for another use.

3. On the prepared baking sheet, toss the sweet potato skins with the olive oil and herbs, then arrange in an even layer. Bake until crispy and fragrant, about 20 minutes. Toss a bit to coat with oil. If needed, return to the oven and bake until they are fully crisp, 3 to 5 minutes more.

4. Sprinkle with flaky salt and serve with the dressing and ketchup alongside for dipping.

roasted pepperoni brussels sprouts

PREP TIME 15 minutes· **COOK TIME** 20 minutes · **TOTAL TIME** 35 minutes · **SERVES** 4

This dish is a little bit different, but don't let that stop you from making it, because these are delicious! Think roasted Brussels sprouts with bacon, which you've probably tried before, but replace the bacon with spicy pepperoni—which I think tastes even better! I started making these a few Thanksgivings back and now they have replaced the classic roasted Brussels sprouts. Everyone gets excited when they hear I'm planning to serve these! Make them for the holidays for sure, but they are also great throughout the fall and winter. We love them as an appetizer on game night, too!

1 pound Brussels sprouts, trimmed and halved lengthwise

3 medium shallots, sliced and separated into rings

3 tablespoons extra-virgin olive oil

Fine pink Himalayan salt and freshly ground black pepper

½ cup freshly grated Parmesan cheese

¼ cup shredded provolone cheese

3 ounces sliced pepperoni

2 tablespoons apple cider vinegar

2 tablespoons fresh thyme leaves

1 tablespoon honey

Crushed red pepper flakes

1. Preheat the oven to 425°F. Line a baking sheet with parchment paper.

2. On the prepared baking sheet, toss together the Brussels sprouts, shallots, olive oil, and a pinch each of salt and pepper. Arrange the Brussels sprouts so all are cut-side down. Sprinkle on the Parmesan and provolone, then layer the pepperoni on top. Roast until the Brussels sprouts are deeply browned and the pepperoni is crisping, about 20 minutes.

3. Meanwhile, in a small bowl, stir together the vinegar, thyme, honey, and a pinch each of red pepper flakes and salt. Taste and adjust the seasonings as needed.

4. Transfer the Brussels sprouts, shallots, and pepperoni to a serving platter. Drizzle the honey mixture over the top and serve warm.

baked honeyed brie

PREP TIME 15 minutes · **COOK TIME** 30 minutes · **TOTAL TIME** 45 minutes, plus chilling time · **SERVES** 6 to 8

My Nonnie passed a few years ago, but I think about her almost every day. I hadn't realized how much of what I do today is influenced by her! Baked Brie was her specialty. She did it SO WELL, and it was the appetizer we'd request at every single one of her dinner parties. Her Brie was always sprinkled with brown sugar and pecans and wrapped in pastry—a true delight. This version is more herby and savory than Nonnie's, but I know she would definitely approve of it. Serve this baked Brie over the holidays—doubling the recipe is always smart whether your crowd is big or small, because guests always devour this one.

1 tablespoon chopped fresh rosemary or thyme

2 garlic cloves, finely chopped or grated

1 (8-ounce) sheet frozen puff pastry, thawed but cold

1 to 2 tablespoons fig preserves

8 ounces Brie, cut into 1-inch cubes

1 cup cubed Gouda or Fontina cheese

2 teaspoons honey

1 large egg, beaten

Coarse sugar, for sprinkling

For Serving

Honey

Freshly ground black pepper

Crusty bread

Crackers

Apple slices

1. Preheat the oven to 425°F. Line a shallow 8- to 10-inch round baking dish or pie plate with parchment paper.

2. In a small bowl, combine the rosemary and garlic. Pinch them together with your fingers until fragrant.

3. Unfold the puff pastry sheet, arranging it flat in the prepared baking dish and letting the excess hang over the sides. Spread the fig preserves in the center of the pastry, leaving about a 1-inch border. Pile the Brie and Gouda on top of the preserves, then sprinkle on the rosemary and garlic mixture. Drizzle with honey. Fold the corners of the pastry over the cheese, mostly covering it. Brush the exposed parts of the pastry with the egg and sprinkle all over with sugar. Chill in the refrigerator for about 10 minutes.

4. Bake until the pastry is deep golden brown and the cheese is bubbling, 25 to 30 minutes.

5. Serve with more honey, black pepper, and your favorite bread, crackers, and/or apple slices—or just with a spoon!

dad's crunchy, cheesy potato skins

PREP TIME 30 minutes · **COOK TIME** 1 hour 20 minutes · **TOTAL TIME** 1 hour 50 minutes · **SERVES 6**

These are my childhood. My dad would make potato skins all the time, usually on nights when my brothers were not eating with us, and it was just Dad, Mom, and me. (Asher wasn't around yet.) Dad always makes them overly cheesy, and he usually leaves them in the oven five minutes too long on purpose because we love these to be CRISPY. Serve the cheesy skins with plain Greek yogurt or, even better, sour cream and lots of green onions. And the bacon bits. You *cannot* skip the bacon bits! I make my own, so they are even yummier!

6 medium russet potatoes

2 tablespoons salted butter, melted

1 garlic clove, finely chopped or grated

2 teaspoons Homemade Seasoned Salt (recipe follows) or store-bought seasoned salt

½ teaspoon chipotle chile powder

½ teaspoon smoked paprika

Fine pink Himalayan salt

2 cups shredded cheddar cheese

For Serving

Bacon slices, cooked and crumbled

Diced or mashed avocado

Chopped fresh cilantro

Sliced green onions

Jalapeños, seeded if desired, and sliced

Plain Greek yogurt or sour cream

1. Preheat the oven to 425°F. Line a baking sheet with parchment paper.

2. Using a fork, prick the potatoes all over. Place directly on the oven rack and bake until tender, about 45 minutes. Remove from the oven and leave the oven set to 425°F. Slice the potatoes in half lengthwise, then let cool.

3. When the potatoes are cool enough to handle, use a spoon to scoop out most of their flesh, leaving about ¼ inch intact, discarding or reserving for another use. Arrange the skins, cut-side up, on the prepared baking sheet.

4. In a small bowl, combine the melted butter, garlic, seasoned salt, chipotle chile powder, paprika, and a pinch of salt. Stir to mix well. Spoon the seasoned butter over each potato skin, dividing evenly.

5. Bake the potato skins until crisp, 15 to 20 minutes. Sprinkle on the cheddar cheese and bake until the cheese is melted and lightly bubbling, 10 to 15 minutes more.

6. Serve immediately topped with lots of crumbled bacon and an assortment of your favorite toppings such as avocado, cilantro, green onions, jalapeños, and/or yogurt.

homemade seasoned salt

———— **MAKES ABOUT ¾ CUP** ————

¼ cup onion powder

¼ cup garlic powder

¼ cup fine pink Himalayan salt

1 tablespoon sweet or smoked paprika

½ teaspoon cayenne pepper

In a small bowl, combine the onion powder, garlic powder, salt, paprika, and cayenne. Stir to mix well. Store in an airtight container at room temperature for up to 12 months.

whipped goat cheese & calabrian chile oil dip

PREP TIME 10 minutes · **COOK TIME** 20 minutes · **TOTAL TIME** 30 minutes · **SERVES** 6

My Nonnie was a pro at making dips, but I never used to even give them the time of day. But now, I try to share at least one new dip every holiday season. I had to give myself a pat on the back after I made this spicy goat cheese dip—using a jar of Calabrian chiles to create something fast but flavorful felt pretty genius at the time. Just be sure to always keep a jar of Calabrian chiles in the pantry and goat cheese in the fridge so you can make it at the last minute! Crusty bread or your favorite crackers are an absolute must for dipping and scooping. A little secret? I think mini pretzel twists are the most delicious vehicle for a dip.

Calabrian Chile Oil

⅓ cup extra-virgin olive oil

1 to 3 tablespoons crushed Calabrian chile peppers, to taste

14 garlic cloves, peeled

Leaves from 4 sprigs fresh thyme

Leaves from 2 sprigs fresh oregano

1 teaspoon freshly ground black pepper

Fine pink Himalayan salt

Whipped Goat Cheese

10 ounces goat cheese, at room temperature

4 ounces cream cheese, at room temperature

2 teaspoons honey

Fine pink Himalayan salt

For Serving

Fresh basil leaves

Crusty bread

Crackers

Crunchy vegetables

1. Make the oil. Preheat the oven to 400°F.

2. In a small baking dish, combine the olive oil, Calabrian chile peppers, garlic, thyme, oregano, black pepper, and a big pinch of salt. Bake until the garlic is golden and the oil is sizzling, about 20 minutes. Remove from the oven and let cool slightly, then use a slotted spoon to transfer the garlic to a cutting board. Finely chop or mash the garlic and stir it into the oil.

3. Meanwhile, make the whipped goat cheese. In a food processor, combine the goat cheese, cream cheese, and honey. Pulse until smooth and creamy, 1 to 2 minutes, stopping a few times to scrape the sides of the bowl with a flexible spatula. Taste and season with salt.

4. Spoon the goat cheese into a serving bowl, then drizzle over the Calabrian chile oil. Top with basil and serve with bread, crackers, and/or vegetables for scooping.

pizza pretzels

PREP TIME 15 minutes · COOK TIME 15 minutes · TOTAL TIME 30 minutes · MAKES 12 pretzels

I made these for the first time many years ago—even before we built our studio space. I think it was 2016. My brother Creighton was looking for a late-afternoon snack. I didn't have anything to cook for him, but I did have pretzels, cheese, and pepperoni. I have no idea why I thought to layer and bake those ingredients together, but I did, and these ended up becoming everyone's favorite snack. Since then, I've added my homemade pizza seasoning blend, and now these are a staple. Large pretzel twists are essential here: they hold the most amount of cheese—and that's what we all want, isn't it?!

$1/2$ cup chopped fresh basil

$1/2$ cup freshly grated Parmesan cheese

$1/3$ cup grated Asiago cheese

2 garlic cloves, finely chopped or grated

1 tablespoon dried thyme

1 tablespoon dried oregano

1 teaspoon crushed fennel seeds

Crushed red pepper flakes

12 Snyder's Olde Tyme pretzels

2 tablespoons salted butter, melted

12 slices provolone cheese (about 4 ounces)

12 slices sandwich-style pepperoni

Warmed marinara sauce, for serving

1. Preheat the oven to 350°F. Line a baking sheet with parchment paper.

2. In a small bowl, combine the basil, Parmesan, Asiago, garlic, thyme, oregano, fennel seeds, and red pepper flakes. Stir to mix well.

3. On the prepared baking sheet, toss the pretzels with the melted butter, then arrange in a single layer. Sprinkle about two-thirds of the herbed cheese mixture over the top.

4. Bake until the cheese is just beginning to melt and the garlic is fragrant, about 5 minutes. Remove the pan from the oven and carefully place a slice of provolone on each pretzel, tearing the slices to fit. Top with a slice of pepperoni.

5. Bake until the cheese is melted and the pepperoni is just beginning to crisp, 10 minutes. Remove and sprinkle with the remaining herbed cheese mixture. Serve warm with marinara sauce for dipping.

apple vanilla chai hot toddy

PREP TIME 5 minutes · **COOK TIME** 5 minutes ·
TOTAL TIME 10 minutes, plus steeping time · **MAKES** 2 drinks

This drink is dedicated to my brother Brendan. I can't even tell you how long he's been asking me to create this, but something made me feel like I should hold off. Now I realize why I did: So I could share the recipe with you, in my coziest cookbook! The chai mixed with the cider and a touch of vanilla creates the most wonderfully warm and spicy mix. It's very lightly sweetened, which I think is essential. Without a ton of added sugar, you can really taste the apples in the cider and the spices in the chai. I make a big pot of this at both Thanksgiving and Christmas, then leave the mix on the stove. It's great for greeting guests as they come in from the cold. It will warm you right up!

½ cup apple cider

2 organic chai tea bags

3 small cinnamon sticks

1 orange slice

Cayenne pepper

Fine pink Himalayan salt

4 ounces (½ cup) bourbon

2 tablespoons fresh lemon juice

1 tablespoon honey

¼ teaspoon pure vanilla extract

For Serving

Apple slices

Star anise

1. In a small saucepan, bring the cider and ½ cup of water to a boil over high heat. Add the tea bags, 1 cinnamon stick, the orange slice, and a small pinch each of cayenne and salt. Remove from the heat, cover, and let steep until very fragrant and darker in color, about 10 minutes.

2. Return the pan to medium heat and warm until steaming. Remove from the heat and add the bourbon, lemon juice, honey, and vanilla.

3. Divide the drink between two mugs. Garnish each one with an apple slice, cinnamon stick (see page 67 for how to light it), and star anise and serve immediately.

make it a mocktail

Omit the bourbon; replace with additional apple cider.

creamy coconut ginger mojito

PREP TIME 10 minutes · **TOTAL TIME** 10 minutes · **MAKES** 1 drink

Mojitos are so underappreciated. I just don't get it. We all need to be making more mojitos, and this is the recipe you have to keep on hand! The coconut, while it's not traditional to the drink, is the secret. It adds a creaminess that works so nicely with the spicy ginger beer and fresh mint. This is one of my favorite cocktails!

Lime Sugar

Zest of 1 lime

2 tablespoons sugar

Flaky sea salt

Mojito

1 lime, quartered

8 fresh mint leaves, plus more for garnish

1 to 2 teaspoons sugar (optional)

1½ ounces (3 tablespoons) white rum

½ ounce (1 tablespoon) coconut rum

Dash of pure vanilla extract

2 ounces (¼ cup) canned coconut cream or cream of coconut

Ginger beer, for topping

1. Make the lime sugar. On a shallow plate, combine the lime zest, sugar, and a pinch of salt.

2. Make the mojito. Rub the rim of a tall glass with a lime wedge. Dip the glass into the lime sugar, pressing to adhere. Fill the glass with ice.

3. In a cocktail shaker, combine 2 lime wedges, the mint, and sugar (if using). Muddle the ingredients together, squishing on them to release their aroma and juices. Add the white rum, coconut rum, and vanilla. Fill with ice and shake vigorously until combined, about 30 seconds. Add the coconut cream and shake for another 30 seconds.

4. Strain into the prepared glass. Top with the ginger beer, then gently stir to combine and dissipate the foam. Garnish with a mint sprig and the remaining lime wedge.

make it a mocktail

Omit the rum; top with an extra squeeze of lime juice and more ginger beer.

aperol pomegranate paloma

PREP TIME 10 minutes · TOTAL TIME 10 minutes, plus standing time · MAKES 1 drink

If you gave me the choice between a margarita and a paloma, I will usually pick the paloma. What I love about a really good paloma is that it's not typically sweetened with a ton of simple syrup, like a margarita can be. Usually just a small amount of syrup, fresh grapefruit juice, lime, tequila, and sparkling water on top. (I do adore a fizzy drink!) It's not fancy, but it's so good! I love this pomegranate version even more, and the shot of Aperol adds another layer of complexity and deliciousness. If you want to be fancy, garnish it with a smoking cinnamon stick—just light the end with a match or lighter, then blow it out. No pressure, you can skip it if the smoke makes you nervous!

Grapefruit Salt

3 tablespoons grapefruit zest (from 2 grapefruit)

2 tablespoons smoked or regular sea salt

2 teaspoons coarse sugar

Paloma

2 grapefruit wedges

2 ounces (¼ cup) tequila or mezcal

1 ounce (2 tablespoons) pomegranate juice

1 ounce (2 tablespoons) fresh grapefruit juice

½ ounce (1 tablespoon) Aperol

1 tablespoon Cinnamon Honey Syrup (recipe follows)

Sparkling water, for topping

Pomegranate seeds, for serving

Cinnamon stick, for garnish (optional)

1. **Make the grapefruit salt.** On a shallow plate, combine the grapefruit zest, salt, and sugar.

2. **Make the paloma.** Rub the rim of a rocks glass with one of the grapefruit wedges. Dip the glass into the salt mixture, pressing to adhere. Fill the glass with ice.

3. Directly into the glass, add the tequila, pomegranate juice, grapefruit juice, Aperol, and cinnamon honey syrup. Stir gently to combine, then top with sparkling water. Garnish with a grapefruit wedge, pomegranate seeds, and a cinnamon stick (if using).

make it a mocktail

Omit the tequila and Aperol; instead, add 1 tablespoon additional pomegranate juice, 1 tablespoon additional grapefruit juice, and 1 tablespoon apple cider vinegar.

cinnamon honey syrup

MAKES ½ CUP

¼ cup honey

2 cinnamon sticks

1 vanilla bean, halved lengthwise and seeds scraped out, or 1 tablespoon pure vanilla extract

In a small saucepan, combine ¼ cup water, the honey, cinnamon sticks, and vanilla bean with the little seeds. Bring to a gentle boil over high heat, then reduce the heat to low and simmer until the cinnamon is fragrant, 1 to 2 minutes. Remove the pan from the heat. Let stand for at least 10 minutes, then discard the cinnamon sticks and transfer to a lidded glass jar. Store in the refrigerator for up to 2 weeks.

lavender gin fizz

PREP TIME 10 minutes · **COOK TIME** 5 minutes ·
TOTAL TIME 15 minutes, plus drying time · **MAKES** 2 drinks

I am always asked where I find inspiration for my recipes and the answer is so simple: the people around me—friends and family. This drink wouldn't have happened if Hailey, my brother Red's girlfriend, had not suggested it. Cocktails are her favorite, so after she had a gin fizz at a restaurant, she told me ALL about it. I did my best to re-create it, and while I don't think this version is exactly like the one she had, she said it's even better. The sugared thyme is so fun—it makes the drink sparkle and is the sweetest garnish. You can use any leftover sugared thyme in a batch of lemony sugar cookies or stirred into a cup of tea. Either would be so delicious!

Sugared Thyme

$\frac{1}{2}$ ounce fresh thyme sprigs

Lavender Honey Syrup
(recipe follows)

Sugar

Gin Fizz

2 ounces ($\frac{1}{4}$ cup) gin

$1\frac{1}{2}$ ounces (3 tablespoons) steeped white or green tea, at room temperature

1 to 3 tablespoons Lavender Honey Syrup (recipe follows)

1 tablespoon fresh lemon juice

2 dashes bitters

1 large egg white

Edible flower petals, for garnish (optional)

1. Make the sugared thyme. Line a baking sheet with parchment paper.

2. Dip the thyme sprigs into the lavender honey syrup just to dampen them, letting the excess drip off. Arrange them on the prepared baking sheet. Sprinkle with sugar, turning the sprigs so they're nicely coated with an even layer of sugar. Let stand at room temperature, uncovered, until they are dry, at least 1 hour or overnight.

3. Make the gin fizz. In a cocktail shaker, combine the gin, tea, lavender honey syrup, lemon juice, bitters, and egg white. Add ice and shake vigorously until foamy, about 1 minute. Strain into two coupe glasses, dividing evenly. Garnish with the sugar thyme and flowers, if desired.

make it a mocktail

Omit the gin; replace with 1 to 2 tablespoons champagne vinegar.

lavender honey syrup

————— **MAKES ABOUT 1 CUP** —————

$\frac{1}{2}$ cup honey

1 rounded tablespoon
dried culinary lavender

2 sprigs fresh thyme

In a small saucepan, combine $\frac{1}{2}$ cup water, the honey, lavender, and thyme. Bring to a low simmer over medium heat, then cook until fragrant, 2 to 3 minutes. Remove the pan from the heat. Let cool slightly, then strain into a lidded glass jar. Store at room temperature for up to 6 months.

cinnamon espresso martini

PREP TIME 5 minutes · **TOTAL TIME** 5 minutes · **MAKES** 1 drink

Espresso martinis are so special to me. I enjoyed my first one at a restaurant called Polo Bar in New York City, where I was celebrating the launch of my first candle collaboration with Snif. (It was Pumpkin Smash, if you remember it!) The table ordered a round of espresso martinis, and now it's tradition—any time I'm having dinner with my Snif family, we always order them to start off the meal! When I mix up my own version at home, I like to use homemade cinnamon syrup, which I think makes them even more special and more delicious. Plus, I love any excuse to garnish a drink with a cinnamon stick!

1½ ounces (3 tablespoons) vodka

1½ ounces (3 tablespoons) Kahlúa

1 ounce (2 tablespoons) brewed espresso, at room temperature

2 to 3 teaspoons Cinnamon Honey Syrup (page 67)

For Serving

Espresso beans

Instant espresso

Cinnamon stick

In a cocktail shaker, combine the vodka, Kahlúa, espresso, and cinnamon honey syrup. Add ice and shake vigorously for 1 minute. Strain into a martini glass. Garnish with espresso beans, a dusting of instant espresso, and a cinnamon stick.

make it a mocktail

Omit the vodka and Kahlúa; replace with an additional 2 ounces brewed espresso.

jalapeño pineapple ginger vodka tonic

PREP TIME 10 minutes · **TOTAL TIME** 10 minutes · **MAKES** 1 drink

It is probably no secret, but I love to combine spicy and sweet, especially when I'm mixing up a cocktail. I think the balance is so interesting, and it's always refreshing. In this cocktail, the small amount of cinnamon is my favorite part. It's unexpected, but the warm spice adds a coziness to the drink that I just adore! You could also use turmeric if you prefer—the color is beautiful, and it adds an earthy flavor—but I think you know I am a cinnamon girl through and through.

4 ounces (½ cup) fresh pineapple juice

2 ounces (¼ cup) vodka

1 ounce (2 tablespoons) fresh lemon or lime juice

1 to 2 jalapeño or serrano pepper slices, plus more for garnish

1 (½-inch) piece fresh ginger, grated

¼ teaspoon ground cinnamon

1 to 2 tablespoons honey

Ginger beer, for topping

Pineapple wedge, for garnish

1. In a cocktail shaker, combine the pineapple juice, vodka, lemon juice, jalapeño, ginger, cinnamon, and honey. Fill with ice and shake until combined, about 1 minute—the longer you shake, the spicier the drink will be.

2. Strain into a tall glass. Top with ginger beer and garnish with a jalapeño slice and pineapple wedge.

make it a mocktail

Omit the vodka; replace with 2 additional tablespoons of pineapple juice plus 1 to 2 tablespoons of apple cider.

soup & salad

the italian chop

PREP TIME 30 minutes · **TOTAL TIME** 30 minutes · **SERVES** 6

Everyone has their go-to recipe for an Italian-style salad. Personally, I think the secret to making a really great version is thinking about it more like an Italian sandwich (minus the bread), so mine includes three kinds of meat, three kinds of cheese, lots of fresh basil, and a homemade dressing. It's fully loaded, so delicious, and (bonus!) my Italian uncle Joe approves.

1 large head romaine lettuce, shredded

1 head radicchio, shredded

6 ounces spicy salami, chopped

3 ounces pepperoni, chopped

3 ounces torn prosciutto

2 cups cherry tomatoes, halved

1 cup mini mozzarella cheese balls

1 cup cubed provolone cheese

1 cup loosely packed fresh basil leaves, plus more for serving

1 cup mixed pitted olives, roughly chopped

1 red bell pepper, chopped

½ cup shaved Parmesan cheese

½ cup sliced pepperoncini

¼ cup chopped dill pickles

¼ cup Homemade Italian Dressing (recipe follows) or store-bought Italian dressing, plus more as needed

1. In a large serving bowl, combine the romaine, radicchio, salami, pepperoni, prosciutto, tomatoes, mozzarella, provolone, basil, olives, bell pepper, Parmesan, pepperoncini, and pickles. Toss to mix well.

2. When ready to serve, pour over the Italian dressing and toss to coat. Add more as desired and top with fresh basil.

homemade italian dressing

———————— **MAKES 1 CUP** ————————

½ cup extra-virgin olive oil

¼ cup apple cider vinegar or champagne vinegar

Juice of 1 lemon

2 tablespoons Dijon mustard

1 rounded tablespoon fig preserves, or 2 teaspoons honey

1 small shallot, finely chopped or grated

2 garlic cloves, finely chopped or grated

½ cup fresh mixed herbs, such as parsley, thyme, and/ or oregano, finely chopped

Fine pink Himalayan salt and freshly ground black pepper

Crushed red pepper flakes, as needed

In a small bowl or lidded jar, combine the olive oil, vinegar, lemon juice, mustard, fig preserves, shallot, garlic, herbs, salt, black pepper, and red pepper flakes. Vigorously whisk or shake to combine well. Taste and adjust the seasonings as needed. Store refrigerated in an airtight container for up to 2 weeks.

sage chicken & apple salad
with harvest vinaigrette

PREP TIME 5 minutes · COOK TIME 25 minutes · TOTAL TIME 30 minutes · SERVES 4 to 6

We all need a salad like this one in our lives. I make this on repeat starting in September when Honeycrisp apples begin making an appearance at my local grocery store. The sweet apples with the salty prosciutto is a combination that is always so delicious and impresses everyone. But it's the pumpkin seeds that I most love here. They add a nice CRUNCH with every bite—and when you make them with a sprinkling of sea salt, they're totally addicting. The dressing is my staple cider-based vinaigrette. I make it with apple butter in the fall, and it tastes so good! Serve this salad for lunch or dinner throughout the fall and winter. It's such a hearty salad that is always satisfying. And so pretty, too!

Salad

1 pound boneless, skinless chicken breasts

1 tablespoon chopped fresh sage

2 tablespoons Homemade Lemon Pepper Seasoning (recipe follows) or store-bought lemon pepper seasoning

Fine pink Himalayan salt

1/3 cup pepitas

1 tablespoon salted butter, melted

1 tablespoon maple syrup

1/2 teaspoon ground cinnamon

1/4 teaspoon cayenne pepper

4 ounces thinly sliced prosciutto, torn

6 cups baby arugula or spring mix

2 Honeycrisp apples, thinly sliced

2 avocados, diced

1/2 cup crumbled feta cheese

Harvest Vinaigrette

1/3 cup extra-virgin olive oil

1/4 cup apple cider vinegar

1 tablespoon Dijon mustard

1 tablespoon Maple Apple Butter (page 195) or store-bought apple butter (optional)

1 tablespoon fresh thyme leaves

2 teaspoons honey or maple syrup

2 teaspoons chopped fresh sage

Fine pink Himalayan salt and freshly ground black pepper

1. Make the salad. Preheat the oven to 400°F. Line a rimmed baking sheet with parchment paper.

2. On one side of the prepared baking sheet, toss the chicken with the chopped sage, lemon pepper seasoning, and salt evenly all over. Bake for 13 to 15 minutes.

3. Meanwhile, in a small bowl, toss together the pepitas, melted butter, maple syrup, cinnamon, cayenne, and a pinch of salt.

4. Carefully remove the baking sheet from the oven and add the coated pepitas to the empty side, spreading them in a single layer. Lay the prosciutto flat around the pepitas. Return the pan to the oven and continue baking until the chicken is cooked through, the pepitas are toasted, and the prosciutto is crisp, about 10 minutes more. Remove from the oven. Transfer the chicken to a cutting board and slice crosswise. Keep it warm.

5. Meanwhile, in a large serving bowl, combine the arugula, apple, and avocado.

6. Make the harvest vinaigrette. In a small bowl or lidded jar, combine the olive oil, vinegar, mustard, apple butter (if using), thyme, honey, and sage. Season with salt and pepper. Vigorously whisk or shake to combine well. Taste and adjust the seasonings as needed.

7. Pour about half of the vinaigrette over the salad and gently toss to coat, adding more dressing as desired. Arrange the chicken, pepitas, and prosciutto over the greens, sprinkle with the feta, and serve.

homemade lemon pepper seasoning

——— MAKES ³/₄ CUP ———

2 tablespoons smoked
or sweet paprika

2 tablespoons garlic powder

2 tablespoons lemon zest

1½ tablespoons fine
pink Himalayan salt

1 tablespoon onion powder

1 tablespoon dried oregano

1 tablespoon dried thyme

1 tablespoon freshly
ground black pepper

2 teaspoons chili powder

In a small bowl, combine the paprika, garlic powder, lemon zest, salt, onion powder, oregano, thyme, black pepper, and chili powder. Stir well to combine. Store at room temperature in an airtight container for up to 6 months.

mean green salad

PREP TIME 25 minutes · **COOK TIME** 5 minutes · **TOTAL TIME** 30 minutes · **SERVES** 4

This is a staple salad. You can make it over the weekend and enjoy it throughout the week, all year round. With lots of shredded cabbage, kale, fresh herbs, and sprouts, it's just the BEST green salad. But it's the homemade tahini Caesar dressing, featuring probably too much grated Parmesan and the most craveable nutty breadcrumbs, that make this salad a standout. The key here is that your salad must be very well dressed. Anything green should be coated in dressing and cheese. It's the only way. If you are making this ahead of time, hold off on adding the dressing and cutting the avocados until you're ready to eat—that way, you avoid a soggy salad and brown avocados, which no one wants!

1½ cups panko breadcrumbs

¼ cup pine nuts (optional)

2 garlic cloves, finely chopped or grated

Fine pink Himalayan salt and freshly ground black pepper

2 tablespoons extra-virgin olive oil

4 cups shredded kale

4 cups shredded green cabbage

1 cup freshly grated Parmesan cheese, plus more for serving

½ cup fresh parsley, chopped

½ cup fresh cilantro, chopped

½ cup Tahini Caesar Dressing (recipe follows) or store-bought Caesar dressing, plus more as needed

2 cups fresh sprouts

2 avocados, sliced

1. Preheat the oven to 425°F.

2. On a baking sheet, combine the panko, pine nuts (if using), garlic, and a pinch each of salt and pepper. Drizzle the olive oil over top and toss to coat. Bake, stirring once, until lightly toasted, about 5 minutes.

3. Meanwhile, in a large bowl, combine the kale, cabbage, ½ cup of the Parmesan, the parsley, and cilantro.

4. To serve, pour the tahini Caesar dressing over the kale, add the remaining ½ cup Parmesan, and toss well, massaging the dressing into the kale. Add more dressing as desired. Top the salad with sprouts, avocado slices, and another handful of Parmesan. Finish with the breadcrumbs.

tahini caesar dressing

───── **MAKES ABOUT 1½ CUPS** ─────

½ cup extra-virgin olive oil

½ cup tahini

½ cup freshly grated Parmesan cheese

¼ cup fresh lemon juice

1 tablespoon Dijon mustard

2 teaspoons vegan Worcestershire sauce

1 to 2 garlic cloves

Fine pink Himalayan salt and freshly ground black pepper

In a blender or food processor, combine the olive oil, tahini, Parmesan, lemon juice, mustard, Worcestershire, garlic, and a pinch each of salt and pepper. Blend on high until smooth, about 1 minute. Add ¼ to ½ cup water to thin the dressing as needed. Taste and adjust the seasonings as needed. Store refrigerated in an airtight container for up to 1 week.

roasted broccoli salad
with nutty breadcrumbs & crispy bacon

PREP TIME 15 minutes · COOK TIME 40 minutes · TOTAL TIME 55 minutes · SERVES 6

Oh my gosh, I love this salad so much. It doesn't feel like a salad—more like the yummiest roasted broccoli dish you can possibly make! As the bacon cooks, its fat renders and the result is the best-tasting roasted broccoli of all time. The breadcrumbs here are super important, too. The addition of hazelnuts turns these breadcrumbs into the perfectly crunchy, slightly sweet topping. This one is great alongside a steak dinner, shared at any holiday table, or just because—I make it all the time!

Salad

6 cups chopped broccoli florets (about 1½ pounds)

3 tablespoons extra-virgin olive oil

2 tablespoons fresh thyme leaves

1 shallot, thinly sliced

Fine pink Himalayan salt and freshly ground black pepper

Crushed red pepper flakes

6 slices thick-cut bacon, chopped

4 thick slices ciabatta bread, cut into small cubes

½ cup hazelnuts or pecans, roughly chopped

1½ cups freshly grated Manchego or Parmesan cheese

1 avocado, diced

Cider Vinaigrette

⅓ cup extra-virgin olive oil

1 medium shallot, finely chopped or grated

2 tablespoons apple cider vinegar

1 tablespoon Maple Apple Butter (page 195) or store-bought apple butter

1 tablespoon fresh thyme leaves

1 teaspoon orange zest

Fine pink Himalayan salt and freshly ground black pepper

Crushed red pepper flakes

1. Make the salad. Preheat the oven to 425°F.

2. On one side of a rimmed baking sheet, combine the broccoli, 2 tablespoons of the olive oil, the thyme, and shallot. Season with salt, black pepper, and red pepper flakes and toss to coat well, then spread into an even layer. Arrange the bacon in an even layer on the opposite side of the pan.

3. Bake until the broccoli is tender and the bacon crispy, about 25 minutes. Using a slotted spoon, transfer both to a large serving bowl. Leave the oven on.

4. To the rendered bacon fat in the pan, add 1 tablespoon olive oil, the ciabatta, and hazelnuts. Season with a pinch each of salt and red pepper flakes and carefully toss to coat. Return to the oven and bake until the bread is golden and toasted, 10 to 15 minutes. If desired, transfer the toasted bread and nuts to a food processor and pulse a few times to create finer crumbs.

5. Meanwhile, make the cider vinaigrette. In a small bowl or lidded jar, combine the olive oil, shallot, vinegar, apple butter, thyme, orange zest, salt, black pepper, and red pepper flakes. Vigorously whisk or shake to combine well. Taste and adjust the seasonings as needed.

6. Pour the vinaigrette over the broccoli and bacon in the bowl and toss to coat well. Add the cheese and avocado and gently toss again. Finish the salad with nutty breadcrumbs before serving.

herby double tomato salad
with burrata

PREP TIME 20 minutes · **TOTAL TIME** 20 minutes · **SERVES** 4 to 6

Well, this salad is just summer in a bowl! Make it when you have the sweetest cherry tomatoes and buckets of fresh basil—both simple but important ingredients. And then for the dressing, the sun-dried tomatoes add a rich, concentrated flavor, which is delicious. I love the contrast of the fresh tomatoes with the sun-dried. Last thing: Please be sure your burrata cheese is at room temperature. That way, it will have the best flavor and creamiest texture. And while you know I think burrata is wonderful in this salad (and in so many dishes), if you can't find it, a fresh mozzarella is a great alternative. Serve the salad with toasted crostini. It's delightful!

Sun-Dried Tomato Dressing

¼ cup finely chopped oil-packed sun-dried tomatoes, plus the jarred oil

Extra-virgin olive oil

¼ cup champagne vinegar

1 tablespoon honey

¼ cup chopped fresh basil

1 tablespoon chopped fresh oregano

Fine pink Himalayan salt and freshly ground black pepper

Crushed red pepper flakes

Salad

3 cups cherry tomatoes, halved

2 Persian cucumbers, diced

1 cup pitted kalamata olives

1 cup chopped fresh herbs, such as basil, oregano, dill, and/or mint

8 ounces burrata cheese, at room temperature

Freshly ground black pepper

1. Make the dressing. Into a spouted measuring cup, pour in the oil from the sun-dried tomato jar, adding olive oil as needed to reach ½ cup total. Whisk in the vinegar and honey until combined. Stir in the chopped sun-dried tomatoes, basil, and oregano. Season with salt, black pepper, and red pepper flakes as needed.

2. Make the salad. In a serving bowl, toss together the tomatoes, cucumbers, olives, and herbs.

3. Pour the sun-dried tomato dressing over the salad and gently toss to coat. Tear the burrata and arrange it around the salad. Season the burrata with black pepper and serve.

spicy sesame ginger roasted chicken salad

PREP TIME 30 minutes · COOK TIME 25 minutes · TOTAL TIME 55 minutes, plus marinating time · SERVES 6 to 8

My family adores this salad. The sesame ginger dressing is what makes it, but I can't lie, the wonton crispies on top always get everyone excited. Most Asian-style chicken salad recipes call for shredded rotisserie chicken, which you can absolutely use here when you are crunched for time. But to really make this salad delicious and give it that homemade touch, I love to make my own spicy roasted chicken, shred it, and toss it with the salad. The gochujang—Korean chili paste—in the marinade adds great flavor. Even my brothers agree: this salad is *good*! They always request a double serving of the chicken, extra dressing (of course), and tons of wonton crispies. They have even said it's totally better than what they would get at a restaurant!

Spicy Roasted Chicken

2 pounds boneless, skinless chicken breasts or thighs

4 garlic cloves, finely chopped or grated

1/3 cup tamari or low-sodium soy sauce

1/4 cup toasted sesame oil

2 to 3 tablespoons gochujang

2 tablespoons rice vinegar

2 teaspoons honey or maple syrup

Fine pink Himalayan salt and freshly ground black pepper

Crushed red pepper flakes

Spicy Sesame Ginger Dressing

1/3 cup toasted sesame oil

1/3 cup tamari or low-sodium soy sauce

1/4 cup honey

1/4 cup toasted sesame seeds

2 tablespoons chopped pickled sushi ginger plus 3 tablespoons jarred pickling liquid

2 to 3 tablespoons gochujang

1 tablespoon orange zest plus 3 tablespoons fresh orange juice

Salad

3 cups shredded Napa or green cabbage (about 8 ounces)

1 medium head romaine lettuce, shredded

1/3 cup slivered almonds or roughly chopped roasted peanuts

1 cup pomegranate seeds

1 orange, suprêmed (see Note)

1 cup fresh cilantro or Thai basil, chopped

For Serving

2 avocados, sliced

3 green onions, thinly sliced

1 (3.5-ounce) bag wonton strips (see Note)

Chili oil

1. Make the chicken. Preheat the oven to 450°F. Line a rimmed baking sheet with parchment paper.

2. In a large bowl or resealable zip-top bag, combine the chicken, garlic, tamari, sesame oil, gochujang, rice vinegar, and honey. Season with salt, black pepper, and red pepper flakes. Let marinate for at least 15 minutes at room temperature or up to overnight in the refrigerator.

3. Transfer the chicken and marinade to the baking sheet. Bake until cooked through, about 25 minutes. Let rest for about 5 minutes, then slice or shred.

4. Meanwhile, make the spicy sesame ginger dressing. In a medium bowl or lidded glass jar, combine the sesame oil, tamari, honey, sesame seeds, ginger and liquid, gochujang, and orange zest and juice. Stir to mix well.

5. Make the salad. In a large serving bowl, combine the chicken, cabbage, lettuce, almonds, pomegranate seeds, orange, and cilantro. Add about half of the dressing and toss to coat. To serve, top with the avocado, green onions, wonton strips, and a drizzle of chili oil.

notes: To suprême the orange (or any other citrus), slice off the top and bottom to create flat surfaces. Use a sharp knife to slice away the skin and white pith, following the shape of the grapefruit and keeping the flesh intact. Working over a bowl to catch the juice, slice lengthwise between each segment and the membrane, adding each segment to the bowl.

To make your own wonton strips, thinly slice 1 package of wonton wrappers and fry them in hot avocado oil until deeply golden and crisp, 1 to 2 minutes. Use a slotted spoon to transfer them to a paper towel–lined plate to drain, and immediately sprinkle them with flaky sea salt.

spicy peanut soup

PREP TIME 25 minutes · **COOK TIME** 30 minutes · **TOTAL TIME** 55 minutes · **SERVES** 6

This is such a cozy, spicy bowl of goodness. It's perfect for fall and winter days when you are craving something warm and packed with flavor and vegetables! It's also vegan and gluten-free, so everyone can enjoy this soup. I use Thai red curry paste to add a ton of flavor while still keeping the number of ingredients to a minimum—it's one of my favorite ingredients to have on hand. Then lots of fresh kale and sweet potatoes join in, which I love with the salty peanuts. It may sound random, but don't knock it until you try it. Totally delicious!

2 tablespoons extra-virgin olive oil

2 small shallots, finely chopped

2 garlic cloves, finely chopped or grated

1 (1-inch) piece fresh ginger, finely chopped or grated

1 jalapeño, seeded, if desired, and finely chopped

3 tablespoons Thai red curry paste

6 cups low-sodium vegetable broth

1 (14-ounce) can unsweetened full-fat coconut milk

1/3 cup creamy peanut butter

2 tablespoons tamari or low-sodium soy sauce

2 medium sweet potatoes, peeled and cubed

1 bunch Tuscan kale, stemmed and roughly chopped

Fine pink Himalayan salt

1/2 cup fresh cilantro, chopped

1 green onion, thinly sliced

2 tablespoons sesame seeds

2 tablespoons chopped salted roasted peanuts

2 tablespoons fresh lime juice, plus more for serving

1. Heat the olive oil in a large Dutch oven over medium heat. When the oil is shimmering, add the shallots, garlic, ginger, and jalapeño. Cook, stirring occasionally, until fragrant, 2 to 3 minutes. Add the curry paste, stirring until well blended and fragrant, another minute more. Stir in the broth, coconut milk, peanut butter, and tamari, mixing well. Add the sweet potatoes and bring to a gentle boil. Reduce the heat to low and simmer until the sweet potatoes are tender, about 15 minutes.

2. Add the kale and cook, stirring occasionally, until wilted, about 5 minutes. Taste and add salt as needed.

3. Meanwhile, in a small bowl, combine the cilantro, green onion, sesame seeds, peanuts, and lime juice. Stir to combine.

4. Ladle the soup into bowls. Top with the cilantro-peanut mixture and another squeeze of lime juice before serving.

creamy turmeric lemon chicken & orzo soup

PREP TIME 20 minutes · **COOK TIME** 40 minutes · **TOTAL TIME** 1 hour · **SERVES** 6

This has become everyone's favorite bowl of chicken soup around here. Creamy, cheesy, and lemony, it's classic but done up with a few special ingredients—turmeric, a Parmesan rind, and lots of fresh herbs—that make it even more delicious. Yes, a Parmesan rind—save yours in a zip-top bag in the freezer! They're edible, too, and are often the most flavorful part of the cheese, so it's no wonder they add a ton of deliciousness to this (and any) soup, where you get all their flavor without having to bite into the hard rind. (Still, you can actually fry them up in a skillet and then eat them!) Serve this soup with crusty bread, or do as my mom does and make a batch of homemade popcorn to sprinkle atop each bowl. It's different but really yummy!

1/4 cup extra-virgin olive oil

8 garlic cloves, chopped

3 medium carrots, chopped

2 to 3 celery stalks, chopped

1 tablespoon chopped fresh sage

1 tablespoon fresh thyme leaves

1 tablespoon chopped fresh rosemary

1/2 teaspoon ground turmeric

Fine pink Himalayan salt and freshly ground black pepper

Crushed red pepper flakes

10 to 12 cups low-sodium chicken broth, or more as needed

1 pound boneless, skinless chicken breasts or thighs

1 Parmesan cheese rind (optional)

1 pound dried orzo

1 bunch Tuscan kale, stemmed and roughly chopped

1 cup whole milk

1 cup freshly grated Parmesan cheese

1/2 cup basil pesto

1 lemon

Chopped fresh dill, for serving

1. Heat the olive oil in a large Dutch oven over medium heat. When the oil is shimmering, add the garlic, carrots, celery, sage, thyme, and rosemary. Cook, stirring, until the vegetables begin to soften and the herbs start to brown, about 5 minutes. Add the turmeric and season with salt, black pepper, and red pepper flakes as needed. Cook, stirring, until fragrant, about 1 minute. Add 10 cups of the broth, the chicken, and Parmesan rind (if using). Increase the heat to high and bring to a boil, then reduce the heat to low and simmer until the chicken is cooked through, 15 to 20 minutes.

2. Using tongs, remove and discard the Parmesan rind. Transfer the chicken to a cutting board. When it is cool enough to handle, tear or shred the meat into bite-size pieces.

3. Add the orzo to the Dutch oven. Return the liquid to a simmer and cook, until the orzo is nearly al dente, about 5 minutes. Add the kale and more chicken broth as needed if the soup is too thick. Cook, stirring occasionally, until the kale is wilted, 5 minutes more. Stir in the milk, Parmesan, pesto, and shredded chicken and cook just until heated through. Taste and add more salt and pepper as needed.

4. Remove from the heat and squeeze in the lemon juice. Ladle the soup into bowls and top with dill before serving.

baked broccoli cheddar-gruyère soup
in bread bowls

PREP TIME 30 minutes · COOK TIME 40 minutes · TOTAL TIME 1 hour 10 minutes · SERVES 4 to 6

If you didn't grow up near a Panera, you may not understand the obsession with this dish (that is, until you try it!). A creamy, cheesy broccoli soup served INSIDE sourdough bread is the coziest, yummiest bowl. It brings back so many childhood memories for me! Mom and I would get this from Panera on the cold, dreary winter days back in Cleveland. It was always such a treat—and aside from baking cookies with my mom, that's one of my most favorite food memories.

4 tablespoons (½ stick) salted butter

4 garlic cloves, chopped

2 teaspoons honey

1 medium yellow onion, diced

1 small carrot, diced

4 celery stalks, chopped

2 tablespoons fresh thyme leaves

Fine pink Himalayan salt and freshly ground black pepper

¼ cup all-purpose flour

½ teaspoon cayenne pepper, plus more as needed

¼ teaspoon freshly grated nutmeg

4 cups low-sodium vegetable or chicken broth

2 cups whole milk

4 cups broccoli florets (about 1 pound)

2 bay leaves

3 cups shredded cheddar cheese

4 to 6 (6-inch) sourdough or pretzel bread bowls, hollowed (see Notes)

2 cups shredded Gruyère cheese

1. Melt the butter in a large Dutch oven over low heat. Add the garlic and cook, stirring, until softened and golden, about 5 minutes. Add the honey and cook until incorporated, about 1 minute. Add the onion, carrot, celery, and thyme and season with salt and pepper. Increase the heat to medium and cook, stirring occasionally, until the vegetables begin to soften, about 5 minutes more.

2. Whisking as you do so, slowly add the flour, cayenne, and nutmeg and cook until the mixture thickens, about 2 minutes. Gradually whisk in the broth, then the milk. Add the broccoli and bay leaves, bring to a simmer and cook, uncovered, until the broccoli is tender, about 10 minutes.

3. Take the pot from the heat. Remove and discard the bay leaves, then use an immersion blender to puree the soup, leaving it a bit chunky. (Alternatively, transfer half of the soup to a blender, puree, then return it to the pot.) Return the soup to low heat and stir in the cheddar, cooking just until it is melted and creamy, 3 to 4 minutes.

4. Meanwhile, place a rack in the top third of the oven and preheat to 400°F.

5. Arrange the hollowed bread bowls on a baking sheet and bake until lightly toasted, about 10 minutes.

6. Ladle the soup into the bread bowls and top with the Gruyère. Bake until the cheese is melted and bubbling, about 10 minutes. Turn on the broiler and broil until the cheese is golden brown, about 1 minute more. Serve immediately.

notes:

To prepare bread bowls, use a long serrated knife to cut a circle through the inside of the bread, taking care not to cut through the bottom, and leaving about one inch attached to the crust all around. Pull out the soft insides with your hands and save for another use— like dipping into this delicious soup or making croutons.

If you can't find small, round loaves of bread for the bowls, pick up sourdough or pretzel rolls and dice them into croutons. Arrange oven-safe bowls on a baking sheet and ladle the soup into the bowls. Top with the croutons and then the Gruyère, and bake, broil, and serve as directed in step 6.

spicy italian sausage tortellini soup

PREP TIME 20 minutes · **COOK TIME** 40 minutes · **TOTAL TIME** 1 hour · **SERVES** 6

One of my favorite soups is a bowl of zuppa Toscana, with Italian sausage and cubed potatoes. In this soup, I swapped out the potatoes for even more delicious, flavorful, and filling cheese tortellini. As you can imagine, it is SO good. I think spicy Italian sausage adds the best flavor, and while you might not think of it this way, a spoonful of basil pesto stirred in just before serving adds a nice pop of brightness to this very cozy bowl. A loaf of warm, crusty bread is a must—I love a fresh ciabatta or go all out with the Cheesy Roasted Shallot Bread (page 47). Yum!

1 pound spicy Italian sausage, casings removed

1 medium yellow onion, chopped

2 garlic cloves, chopped

2 tablespoons tomato paste

2 tablespoons fresh thyme leaves

2 tablespoons Italian seasoning

Fine pink Himalayan salt and freshly ground black pepper

2 carrots, chopped

4 celery stalks, chopped

6 cups low-sodium chicken broth

4 cups roughly chopped kale

$1/2$ cup whole milk or heavy cream

$1/4$ cup basil pesto

1 pound fresh cheese tortellini

$1/2$ cup freshly grated Parmesan cheese, plus more for serving

Chopped fresh basil, for serving

1. Heat a large Dutch oven over medium heat. When the pot is hot, add the sausage and onion. Cook, breaking up the sausage with a spoon, until some fat has rendered and the meat has browned all over, about 8 minutes. Add the garlic, tomato paste, thyme, Italian seasoning, salt, and pepper. Cook, stirring, until fragrant and the tomato paste is dark brick red, 1 to 2 minutes more.

2. Add the carrots and celery. Cook, stirring, until they begin to soften, about 5 minutes. Pour in the broth. Bring to a simmer and cook until the vegetables are tender and the flavors melded, 10 to 15 minutes.

3. Stir in the kale, milk, and pesto and cook until the kale is slightly wilted, about 2 minutes. Add the tortellini and Parmesan and cook until the tortellini is cooked and the cheese is melted, 3 minutes more.

4. To serve, ladle the soup into bowls and top with more Parmesan and fresh basil.

thai curry–inspired chicken & rice soup

PREP TIME 20 minutes · **COOK TIME** 30 minutes · **TOTAL TIME** 50 minutes · **SERVES** 4 to 6

My mom and little sister love chicken soup—a classic bowl with lots of noodles. But sometimes my mom would make a very basic pot of chicken soup, then add leftover rice instead of the noodles. Asher and I both remember it being so cozy and comforting. I took her idea and used rice here—cooking it in the pot along with everything else—and I built the flavors to more of a Thai-inspired base, with Thai red curry paste and coconut milk to make it creamier. The result is SO flavorful! If you want to do it my mom's way with leftover rice, you can make this on a Sunday and enjoy it throughout the week, adding rice to each serving.

1 pound boneless, skinless chicken thighs

6 cups low-sodium chicken broth

4 garlic cloves, finely chopped or grated

1 (2-inch) piece fresh ginger, chopped or grated

2 shallots, chopped

¼ cup fresh lime juice (from 3 limes)

¼ cup Thai red curry paste

2 tablespoons fish sauce

1 tablespoon creamy peanut butter

1 teaspoon ground turmeric

1 cup jasmine rice

1 (14-ounce) can unsweetened full-fat coconut milk

5 ounces shredded kale or baby spinach

⅓ cup fresh Thai basil or cilantro, chopped, plus a few sprigs for serving

Fine pink Himalayan salt

For Serving

Thinly sliced green onions

Chopped peanuts

Sesame seeds

Pickled sushi ginger

1. In a large Dutch oven, combine the chicken, chicken broth, garlic, ginger, shallots, lime juice, curry paste, fish sauce, peanut butter, and turmeric. Stir in the rice. Place over high heat and bring to a boil, then reduce the heat to low and cook, stirring occasionally, until the chicken is cooked through, 15 to 20 minutes.

2. Using tongs or two forks, remove the chicken to a cutting board, shred it, and return it to the pot. Stir in the coconut milk, kale, and Thai basil. Cook, stirring, until the greens are wilted and the flavors are melded, about 2 minutes. Taste and add salt as needed.

3. Ladle the soup into bowls. Top with Thai basil sprigs, green onions, peanuts, sesame seeds, and pickled ginger before serving.

loaded potato soup
with salsa verde

PREP TIME 15 minutes · **COOK TIME** 50 minutes · **TOTAL TIME** 1 hour 5 minutes · **SERVES** 6

I was never really interested in potato soup—it just didn't sound all that amazing to me, so I never ordered it out or made it at home. That is, until my cousin Maggie told me all about a potato soup she loves to order in Lakewood, Ohio. She described it as creamy but a little spicy—and she thinks the secret is a really good sharp cheddar cheese, plus so much crispy bacon on top. I took notes and finally tried it . . . and it is SO good. I love to use salsa verde to add flavor and spice, and then, as with any potato dish, the toppings are most important. Avocado, dollops of yogurt, so many green onions, and lots of those crispy homemade bacon bits. Make this tonight!

6 slices thick-cut bacon, chopped

1 medium yellow onion, chopped

4 garlic cloves, chopped

1 jalapeño, seeded, if desired, and chopped

2 teaspoons ground cumin

1 teaspoon smoked paprika

1/2 teaspoon chili powder

Fine pink Himalayan salt and freshly ground black pepper

4 cups low-sodium chicken broth

4 medium russet potatoes, peeled and chopped

2 cups whole milk

1/3 cup salsa verde

1/3 cup plain Greek yogurt or sour cream, plus more for serving

1 cup shredded cheddar cheese, plus more for serving

1/4 cup chopped fresh cilantro, plus more for serving

Diced avocado, for serving

Thinly sliced green onions, for serving

1. Place the bacon in a Dutch oven over medium heat and cook until the fat is rendered and the bacon is crispy, 6 to 8 minutes. Using a slotted spoon, transfer the bacon to a paper towel–lined plate, reserving the fat in the pot.

2. Stir the onion into the bacon fat and cook over medium-high heat until it begins to soften, about 5 minutes. Add the garlic, jalapeño, cumin, paprika, and chili powder. Season with salt and pepper. Cook, stirring, until fragrant, about 1 minute.

3. Add the chicken broth and potatoes. Increase the heat to high and bring to a boil. Partially cover the pan, reduce the heat to medium-low, and simmer until the potatoes are very soft, 20 to 30 minutes. Working right in the pot, use a potato masher or fork to mash some of the potatoes; I like to leave my soup a bit chunky.

4. Stir in the milk, salsa verde, and yogurt. Cook, stirring occasionally, until well incorporated and warmed through, about 5 minutes. Add the cheese and stir until melted, about 1 minute. Remove from the heat and stir in the cilantro.

5. To serve, ladle the soup into bowls and top with yogurt, cheese, cilantro, avocado, green onions, and bacon.

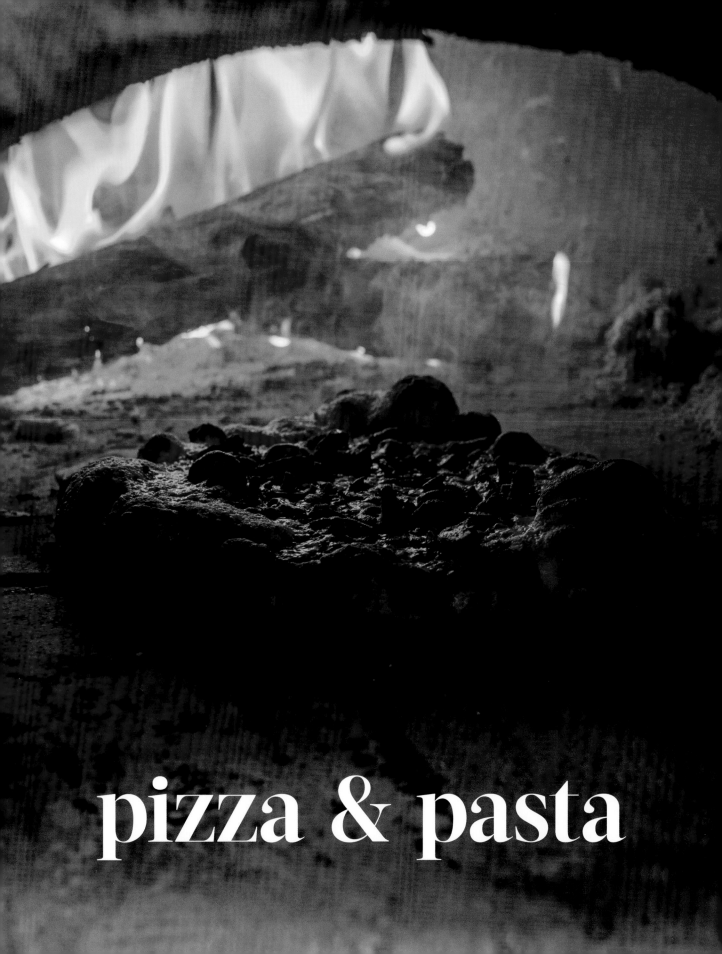

pizza & pasta

pickled pepper pepperoni pizza

PREP TIME 15 minutes · **COOK TIME** 15 minutes · **TOTAL TIME** 30 minutes · **SERVES** 4

This pizza reminds me a lot of the one my dad would make when we were growing up. He'd use a store-bought, prebaked crust that, in retrospect, tasted more like cardboard than pizza crust—but it was fine because the toppings made up for it: lots of olive oil, garlic, dried oregano, so many red pepper flakes, and a pile of cheese, and then he'd finish it with way too many pepperoni slices and cover the surface with thinly sliced bell peppers. The peppers were my favorite part! I took his idea and made it just a touch more delicious. You guys, these pickled peppers are SPECIAL. First you char the bell peppers all over, then steam them to remove the skin. After that, they're tossed in an oil-and-vinegar pickling sauce. Complete game changer—try them on anything and everything!

Flour, for dusting

½ pound pizza dough, at room temperature

Extra-virgin olive oil, for brushing

3 garlic cloves, finely chopped or grated

1 teaspoon smoked paprika

1 teaspoon dried oregano

Crushed red pepper flakes

⅓ cup pitted kalamata olives, sliced

2 tablespoons sliced pepperoncini

¾ cup shredded low-moisture whole-milk mozzarella cheese

¾ cup shredded provolone cheese

½ cup freshly grated Parmesan cheese

4 ounces pepperoni, sliced

1½ cups Pickled Roasted Peppers (recipe follows) or jarred roasted red peppers, sliced

Torn fresh basil, for serving

1. Preheat the oven to 450°F. Line a baking sheet with parchment paper.

2. On a lightly floured work surface, roll out the dough to ¼-inch thickness. Carefully transfer the dough to the prepared baking sheet.

3. Generously brush the crust all over with olive oil. Add the garlic, paprika, oregano, and a pinch or two of red pepper flakes. Scatter over the olives and pepperoncini. Add the mozzarella, provolone, and Parmesan, then arrange the pepperoni on top.

4. Bake until the crust is golden and the cheese is bubbling, 10 to 15 minutes. Add the pickled roasted peppers and bake until they are hot, 5 minutes more. Top with basil, then slice and serve.

pickled roasted peppers

——— **MAKES ABOUT 3½ CUPS** ———

⅔ cup extra-virgin olive oil

¼ cup red wine vinegar

¼ cup balsamic vinegar

¼ cup chopped fresh basil

1 tablespoon chopped fresh oregano

3 garlic cloves, thinly sliced, plus 3 roughly chopped

2 teaspoons honey

Crushed red pepper flakes

Fine pink Himalayan salt and freshly ground black pepper

4 red, orange, and/or yellow bell peppers

In a large bowl or 1-quart glass jar, combine the olive oil, red wine vinegar, balsamic vinegar, basil, oregano, garlic, honey, and red pepper flakes, and season with salt and pepper. Turn a gas burner to medium-high. Using heatproof tongs and working with one at a time, cook each bell pepper directly over the flame, turning as necessary until charred all over, 7 to 9 minutes total. Transfer to a clean bowl and cover completely with a plate; the steam will loosen the skins. Let stand for about 15 minutes, then rub off the blackened pepper skin. Cut four sides from each pepper, leaving behind the stem, membrane, and seeds. Add the peppers to the oil mixture, submerging them completely. Let marinate at room temperature for at least 15 minutes or up to 2 weeks refrigerated in an airtight container.

jalapeño buffalo chicken pizza

PREP TIME 15 minutes · **COOK TIME** 15 minutes · **TOTAL TIME** 30 minutes · **SERVES** 4

I have the deepest love for this pizza. It reminds me so much of the buffalo chicken pizza I'd order back in Ohio. It was a rare night when we ordered in pizza, but any time I could convince my parents, that's the one I would get. It always came with sliced jalapeños and lots of buffalo sauce, plus a side of ranch for dipping. SO GOOD. I did my best to re-create that version, and even though my memories of it are epic, I know this one is even better. Be generous with the buffalo sauce—you really want the pizza to be dripping with it. That doesn't sound all that appetizing, but trust me, it's YUMMY. My brothers stand by this recipe; they say it's one of my best. That should tell you a lot! Make it for a game day and watch everyone love it!

1 cup diced cooked chicken

4 ounces cream cheese, at room temperature

1/3 cup plus 2 tablespoons Homemade Buffalo Sauce (page 176) or store-bought buffalo sauce

1 jalapeño, seeded, if desired, and chopped

1/4 cup fresh cilantro, chopped, plus more for serving

2 tablespoons fresh dill, chopped

2 green onions, sliced, plus more for serving

Flour, for dusting

1/2 pound pizza dough, at room temperature

1 cup shredded low-moisture whole-milk mozzarella cheese

1 cup shredded Monterey Jack cheese

1/2 cup freshly grated Parmesan or Asiago cheese

Homemade Ranch Dressing (recipe follows) or store-bought ranch dressing, for serving

1. Preheat the oven to 450°F. Line a baking sheet with parchment paper.

2. In a medium bowl, combine the chicken, cream cheese, 1/3 cup of the buffalo sauce, the jalapeño, cilantro, dill, and green onions. Stir to mix well.

3. On a lightly floured work surface, roll out the dough to 1/4-inch thickness. Carefully transfer the dough to the prepared baking sheet.

4. Scatter the chicken mixture evenly over the dough, leaving a 1-inch border. Add the mozzarella, Monterey Jack, and Parmesan, then drizzle with the remaining 2 tablespoons buffalo sauce.

5. Bake until the crust is golden and the cheese is bubbling, 15 to 20 minutes. Remove from the oven and top with green onions and cilantro. Slice and serve with the ranch dressing drizzled over the top and/or alongside for dipping.

homemade ranch dressing

— **MAKES 1 1/2 CUPS** —

1/2 cup sour cream or plain Greek yogurt

1/2 cup mayonnaise

1/3 cup freshly grated Parmesan cheese

1 tablespoon dried chives

2 teaspoons dried dill

1 teaspoon garlic powder

1 teaspoon onion powder

1/4 cup pickled jalapeños, chopped, plus 2 tablespoons brine

Fine pink Himalayan salt and freshly ground black pepper

In a medium bowl, combine the sour cream, mayo, Parmesan, chives, dill, garlic powder, onion powder, jalapeños, and their brine. Season with salt and pepper. Stir to mix well, adding water as needed until your desired consistency is reached. Taste and adjust the seasonings as needed. Store refrigerated in an airtight container for up to 2 weeks.

four cheese balsamic mushroom pizza

PREP TIME 10 minutes · **COOK TIME** 15 minutes · **TOTAL TIME** 25 minutes · **SERVES** 4

To me, mushroom pizza is such a staple. Yes, pepperoni with lots of basil will forever be my favorite, but a pie with gooey cheese and a ton of mushrooms can be just as craveable and delicious. Here, I toss the mushrooms with balsamic vinegar, which tastes SO good with the mix of creamy, tangy cheeses (four of them!). If you can, a good-quality balsamic is worth getting—I love one with a fruity undertone like Brightland or Flamingo Estate, which are my favorites. Red pepper flakes are also a must on this pizza; their heat balances the sweetness from the balsamic. Sometimes I add a small handful of spinach or basil leaves to the mushrooms.

1 cup sliced cremini or shiitake mushrooms

1 shallot, chopped

1 garlic clove, finely chopped or grated

3 tablespoons balsamic vinegar, plus more for serving

2 tablespoons extra-virgin olive oil

1 tablespoon fresh thyme

Fine pink Himalayan salt and freshly ground black pepper

Crushed red pepper flakes (optional)

Flour, for dusting

½ pound pizza dough, at room temperature

1 cup shredded Gouda cheese

2 ounces goat cheese, crumbled

½ cup shredded Havarti cheese

¼ cup freshly grated Parmesan cheese

1. Preheat the oven to 450°F. Line a baking sheet with parchment paper.

2. In a medium bowl, combine the mushrooms, shallot, garlic, balsamic, olive oil, and thyme. Season with salt, black pepper, and red pepper flakes (if using).

3. On a lightly floured work surface, roll out the dough to ¼-inch thickness. Carefully transfer the dough to the prepared baking sheet.

4. Scatter half the mushroom mixture evenly over the dough, leaving a 1-inch border. Add the Gouda, goat cheese, Havarti, and Parmesan, then spoon over the remaining mushroom mixture.

5. Bake until the crust is golden and the cheese is bubbling, 15 to 20 minutes. Drizzle with more balsamic, then slice and enjoy!

spicy pepperoni pesto pizza
with honey drizzle

PREP TIME 15 minutes · **COOK TIME** 15 minutes · **TOTAL TIME** 30 minutes · **SERVES** 4

Hands down, pepperoni pizza will always be my favorite. It's classic for a reason and I LOVE it—nothing beats it! This recipe is just a bit more dressed up than what you might be used to, with the addition of spicy sliced pepperoncini and pesto in place of the usual red sauce. Then three kinds of cheese and, you won't be surprised, I cover the surface in thinly sliced pepperoni. You can go big or small for the pepperoni, but be sure to really layer them on. Don't skimp! Then, my super delicious special touch: sesame seeds on the crust. I think they add the best flavor and tiniest bit of crunch. You have to try it!

Flour, for dusting

$\frac{1}{2}$ pound pizza dough, at room temperature

Extra-virgin olive oil

1 tablespoon sesame seeds

$\frac{1}{3}$ cup basil pesto

2 tablespoons sliced pepperoncini

$\frac{1}{2}$ cup shredded low-moisture whole-milk mozzarella cheese

$\frac{1}{2}$ cup shredded provolone cheese

$\frac{1}{4}$ cup freshly grated Parmesan cheese

1 teaspoon dried oregano

3 ounces pepperoni, sliced

For Serving

Dried oregano

Torn fresh basil

Honey

1. Preheat the oven to 450°F. Line a baking sheet with parchment paper.

2. On a lightly floured work surface, roll out the dough to $\frac{1}{4}$-inch thickness. Carefully transfer the dough to the prepared baking sheet.

3. Lightly brush the crust all over with olive oil, then sprinkle the crust with the sesame seeds. Spread the pesto over the dough, leaving a 1-inch border. Arrange the pepperoncini over the top. Add the mozzarella, provolone, and Parmesan, finishing with the oregano and then pepperoni.

4. Bake until the crust is golden and the cheese is bubbling, 15 to 20 minutes. Top with another pinch of dried oregano and fresh basil, then drizzle generously with honey. Slice and enjoy!

cait's prosciutto pizza

PREP TIME 15 minutes · COOK TIME 50 minutes · TOTAL TIME 1 hour 5 minutes · SERVES 4

I love nothing more than cooking food for my friends and family—and this pizza is for Cait, my friend since we were teenagers. It's our girls'-night-in pizza, best enjoyed with a few tall candles and your favorite bottle of whatever you drink—we're into Lambrusco. The specialness behind this particular pizza lies with the roasted garlic, pumpkin, and of course, the prosciutto. The garlic becomes sweet once it's roasted, so pairing it with something like a nutty pumpkin makes for an absolutely delicious combination. Finally, the prosciutto adds a perfect, contrasting saltiness that really makes you shout YUM with each bite.

2 cups 1-inch-cubed pumpkin or butternut squash (from 1 small)

8 garlic cloves

6 tablespoons extra-virgin olive oil

Fine pink Himalayan salt and freshly ground black pepper

Crushed red pepper flakes

2 teaspoons honey, plus more for serving

Flour, for dusting

½ pound pizza dough, at room temperature

1 cup shredded low-moisture whole-milk mozzarella cheese

½ cup shredded Gouda or fontina cheese

1 cup chopped fresh spinach

3 ounces thinly sliced prosciutto, torn

2 teaspoons chopped fresh sage or thyme leaves

Fresh basil, for serving

1. Preheat the oven to 450°F. Line a baking sheet with parchment paper.

2. On the prepared baking sheet, toss together the pumpkin, garlic, and 3 tablespoons of the olive oil. Season with salt, black pepper, and red pepper flakes. Bake until the garlic is soft and the pumpkin is fork-tender, 15 to 20 minutes. Leave the oven on.

3. Let cool until it can be handled. Gently squeeze the roasted garlic into a medium bowl. Add the remaining 3 tablespoons olive oil, the honey, and red pepper flakes. Mash with a fork until well combined.

4. On a lightly floured work surface, roll out the dough to ¼-inch thickness. Carefully transfer the dough to the prepared baking sheet.

5. Spread the honeyed garlic over the dough, leaving a 1-inch border (you may not need to use all of it). Top with the mozzarella and Gouda and then the spinach. Arrange the roasted pumpkin on top, then the prosciutto.

6. Bake until the crust is golden and the cheese is bubbling, 15 to 20 minutes. Top with the sage, basil, and more red pepper flakes. Drizzle with honey before slicing and serving.

gochujang margherita pizza

PREP TIME 15 minutes · **COOK TIME** 15 minutes · **TOTAL TIME** 30 minutes · **SERVES** 4

This pizza shocks everyone I serve it to—but in a good way. I use gochujang as the base, which is a Korean chili paste you can find online and in Asian markets. It adds a spicy, sweet, tangy taste that's just delectable. No one quite knows what the flavor is because it's softened a bit from all the cheese on top—but they definitely know it's yummy. Lots of cherry tomatoes and basil complete this perfect twist on a classic margherita! It's fun to make in the summer when the farmers' markets and gardens are bursting.

$3/4$ cup cherry tomatoes

2 garlic cloves, finely chopped or grated

1 medium shallot, sliced

$1/4$ cup extra-virgin olive oil

1 tablespoon fish sauce

1 teaspoon dried oregano

1 teaspoon honey, plus more for serving

Fine pink Himalayan salt and freshly ground black pepper

Crushed red pepper flakes

Flour, for dusting

$1/2$ pound pizza dough, at room temperature

2 tablespoons gochujang

1 cup shredded Gouda cheese

1 cup shredded mozzarella cheese

6 to 8 fresh basil leaves

1. Preheat the oven to 450°F. Line a baking sheet with parchment paper.

2. In a medium bowl, combine the tomatoes, garlic, shallot, olive oil, fish sauce, oregano, and honey. Season with salt, black pepper, and red pepper flakes and toss gently to coat.

3. On a lightly floured work surface, roll out the dough to $1/4$-inch thickness. Carefully transfer the dough to the prepared baking sheet.

4. Spread the gochujang evenly over the dough, leaving a 1-inch border. Spoon the tomato mixture over the gochujang, then scatter the Gouda and mozzarella over the top.

5. Bake until the crust is golden and the cheese is bubbling, about 15 minutes. Top with the basil leaves, slice, and serve with honey.

ciabatta pizza

PREP TIME 10 minutes · **COOK TIME** 15 minutes · **TOTAL TIME** 25 minutes · **SERVES** 6

This recipe reminds me of a pizza bagel, which I would sometimes make after school when my family lived in Cleveland. My mom kept our freezer stocked with bagels, and I used them to make sandwiches and quick pizzas in the microwave. But the ciabatta is a big improvement. It's one of my favorite types of breads—it's so airy inside, and I love when those air pockets get filled with sauce and cheese. Can you say YUM? Be sure you cook these pizzas until the cheese is super melty and the pepperoni on top begins to crisp, which allows sufficient time for the bread underneath to get toasty. Then top it all with fresh basil. It comes together super fast and is pretty much perfect.

¾ cup freshly grated Parmesan cheese

½ cup chopped fresh basil, plus torn basil leaves for serving

¼ cup chopped fresh oregano

1 to 2 garlic cloves, finely chopped or grated

1 teaspoon onion powder

1 teaspoon fennel seeds

1 teaspoon sesame seeds

1 (1-pound) loaf ciabatta bread or baguette, halved lengthwise

2 cups marinara sauce

1 cup shredded low-moisture whole-milk mozzarella

1 cup shredded provolone cheese

½ cup shredded cheddar cheese

3 ounces pepperoni, sliced

Extra-virgin olive oil, for drizzling

1. Preheat the oven to 425°F.

2. In a small bowl, combine ¼ cup of the Parmesan, the basil, oregano, garlic, onion powder, fennel seeds, and sesame seeds.

3. Arrange the ciabatta halves on a baking sheet, cut sides up. Spread with the marinara sauce, dividing evenly, then add the mozzarella, provolone, cheddar, and remaining ½ cup Parmesan. Sprinkle over the basil mixture, then arrange the pepperoni on top. Drizzle with olive oil.

4. Bake until the cheese is bubbling, about 15 minutes. Top with more fresh basil, then slice and serve.

spinach calzones
with garlic butter

PREP TIME 25 minutes · COOK TIME 25 minutes · TOTAL TIME 50 minutes · SERVES 6

Spinach calzones always make me think of my Nonnie. The first time I tried a calzone was with her, on one of our summertime girls-only trips to Florida. Nonnie loved a good pizza or pasta dinner. One night, she took me to an Italian restaurant and we both ordered the white spinach calzones. I remember them being so delicious, heavy on the white sauce and with just the right amount of spinach (as in, not too much!). And the tops were slathered with garlic Parmesan butter. It was heavenly. I can't believe it's taken me this long to re-create the recipe!

Calzones

1 cup ricotta cheese

¾ cup basil pesto

2 large eggs yolks

Fine pink Himalayan salt and freshly ground black pepper

Crushed red pepper flakes

1 pound pizza dough, at room temperature

Flour, for dusting

2 cups baby spinach, chopped

½ cup shredded provolone cheese

½ cup shredded Gouda cheese

Garlic Butter

4 tablespoons (½ stick) salted butter

1 garlic clove, finely chopped or grated

2 tablespoons fresh thyme leaves

¼ cup freshly grated Parmesan cheese

1 tablespoon sesame seeds

Freshly ground black pepper

1. Make the calzones. Preheat the oven to 450°F. Line a baking sheet with parchment paper.

2. In a medium bowl, stir together the ricotta, ¼ cup of the pesto, and the egg yolks. Season with salt, black pepper, and red pepper flakes.

3. Divide the pizza dough into 2 balls. On a lightly floured surface, roll out each ball of dough into a large circle, about ¼ inch thick.

4. Leaving a ½-inch border, spread one half of each round with ¼ cup of pesto, then top the pesto with half of the pesto-ricotta mixture, spreading it evenly. Top each with equal portions of the spinach, provolone, and Gouda.

5. Using a pastry brush, brush the border of the dough with water. Fold over the unfilled sides of the dough rounds to enclose the filling. Use the tines of a fork to seal the edges. Cut a 2-inch slit in the top of each calzone. Transfer to the prepared baking sheet and bake until the tops of the calzones are golden brown, 20 to 25 minutes.

6. Meanwhile, make the garlic butter. Melt the butter in a small skillet over medium heat. Add the garlic and thyme and cook until fragrant, about 1 minute. Remove from the heat and stir in the Parmesan and sesame seeds. Season with black pepper.

7. Serve the calzones with garlic butter drizzled on top or alongside for dipping.

effortless pasta bake

PREP TIME 15 minutes · **COOK TIME** 45 minutes · **TOTAL TIME** 1 hour · **SERVES** 8

In the fall and winter, I love to make baked pasta dishes. They are easy to prepare ahead of time, and they feel extra cozy to me. I think it's because, like my dad, I always top any baked pasta with a little too much cheese—but in my mind, there is no other way to do it! The best part about this pasta is that you don't have to boil the pasta! Just mix all the ingredients in a dish, then bake. That's it! Nothing fussy or fancy. I start by pre-roasting the cherry tomatoes, but if you don't have fresh tomatoes, you can skip this step and add a few tablespoons of sun-dried tomatoes to boost the flavor. Make this when you're serving guests, and pair it with the Mean Green Salad (page 82). Such an easy meal to entertain with!

3 cups cherry tomatoes

$1/2$ cup extra-virgin olive oil

6 garlic cloves, roughly chopped

3 tablespoons Homemade Italian Seasoning (page 128) or store-bought Italian seasoning

Fine pink Himalayan salt and freshly ground black pepper

Crushed red pepper flakes

1 pound short-cut pasta, such as orzo or macaroni

$1/2$ cup pitted Kalamata olives, roughly chopped

$1/3$ cup chopped fresh basil, plus more for serving

2 to 3 tablespoons sliced pepperoncini

2 cups shredded mozzarella cheese

4 ounces sliced pepperoni

2 bell peppers, any color, thinly sliced

1. Preheat the oven to 400°F.

2. In a 9 x 13-inch baking dish, combine the cherry tomatoes, olive oil, garlic, Italian seasoning, salt, black pepper, and red pepper flakes. Bake until the tomatoes begin to burst, about 10 minutes. Pull the pan out of the oven (leave the oven on) and add the pasta, olives, basil, and pepperoncini. Pour in 2 cups of water and stir to combine. Top with the mozzarella, pepperoni, and bell peppers.

3. Return to the oven to bake, until the sauce is bubbling and the cheese is melted, 35 minutes more.

4. Top with lots of fresh basil and extra red pepper flakes. Serve family style.

sage brown butter lemon pasta
with zucchini

PREP TIME 15 minutes · COOK TIME 15 minutes · TOTAL TIME 30 minutes · SERVES 4

Sometimes the simplest pastas are the most special, and that's the case with this dish. The sauce is a garlicky alfredo sauce—the same one my dad made when I was growing up. I made it my own with the addition of crispy sage and brown butter, and I snuck some veggies in here, too. I like to make this with spaghetti to match the length and shape of the zucchini, but any long cut of pasta works well. Whatever you do, don't skip the prosciutto. I love the way its salty crunch contrasts with this very creamy pasta. In the summer, add fresh basil and cherry tomatoes!

Fine pink Himalayan salt

1 pound spaghetti

4 ounces torn prosciutto

6 tablespoons salted butter

12 fresh sage leaves

3 garlic cloves, chopped

Freshly ground black pepper

1 cup heavy cream

1 cup freshly grated Parmesan cheese, plus more for serving

1/2 cup freshly grated pecorino cheese, plus more for serving

1 cup shredded zucchini (from 1 small)

1 tablespoon fresh lemon juice

1. Bring a large pot of salted water to a boil over high heat. Add the spaghetti and cook until al dente according to package directions. Reserve 1/2 cup pasta cooking water, then drain.

2. Meanwhile, in a large skillet over medium-high heat, cook the prosciutto, stirring occasionally, until it is crispy, about 5 minutes. Transfer the prosciutto to a plate.

3. Add the butter, sage, and garlic to the same skillet. Season with salt and 1 1/2 teaspoons pepper. Cook, stirring, until the sage is crisp and the butter is browning, about 5 minutes. Remove a few sage leaves to reserve for serving.

4. Pour in the cream, then add the Parmesan and pecorino. Stir to melt the cheese, then add the cooked spaghetti and zucchini and toss to coat well. If needed, gradually add the reserved pasta cooking water and toss again to reach your desired texture; the sauce should lightly coat the pasta without being runny. Remove from the heat and stir in the lemon juice. Top with the crispy prosciutto and reserved sage leaves and serve immediately with more cheese and pepper, as desired.

sheet pan mac & cheese
with all the crispy edges

PREP TIME 15 minutes · **COOK TIME** 25 minutes · **TOTAL TIME** 40 minutes · **SERVES** 8

When I was a kid, way back when my family still lived in Cleveland, my mom used to buy Stouffer's Frozen Macaroni & Cheese. Whenever I would pop one into the microwave, I loved how the corners would get a little overcooked and become crispy. You know what I am talking about! I remember them being so delicious. Well, this is my homemade version of that mac and cheese. I wanted crispy cheese edges, but lots of yummy, creamy cheese sauce in the middle. And to do that, you just bake it on a sheet pan, which has a lot more space around the edges than a deep baking pan. In my mind, this is the perfect version of mac and cheese—you get all the best parts!

Fine pink Himalyan salt

1 pound short-cut pasta, such as macaroni

2 cups whole milk

1 tablespoon arrowroot or cornstarch

4 ounces cream cheese, at room temperature

1 tablespoon Dijon mustard

2 cups shredded sharp cheddar cheese

1 cup shredded Monterey Jack cheese

3 tablespoons salted butter

1 teaspoon garlic powder

1 teaspoon onion powder

1 teaspoon sweet or smoked paprika

1/4 teaspoon cayenne pepper

Freshly ground black pepper

2 cups shredded Colby Jack cheese

For Serving

Chopped fresh herbs

Thinly sliced green onions

1. Preheat the oven to 425°F.

2. Bring a large pot of salted water to a boil over high heat. Add the pasta and cook until very al dente, 4 to 5 minutes. Drain, then immediately return the hot pasta to the hot pot (leave the heat off).

3. In a spouted measuring cup, whisk together the milk and arrowroot. Add the cream cheese and mustard to the hot pasta and stir well until the cream cheese is melted and the pasta is well coated. Pour the milk mixture over the pasta, and add the cheddar cheese, Monterey Jack cheese, butter, garlic powder, onion powder, paprika, and cayenne. Season with salt and pepper. Stir to combine to melt some of the cheese.

4. Transfer the pasta to a rimmed baking sheet. Sprinkle the Colby Jack cheese over the top. Bake until the cheese is melted and the edges are crisping, 15 to 20 minutes.

5. To serve, top with fresh herbs and green onions, then dig in and enjoy!

cacio e pepe ravioli

PREP TIME 10 minutes · **COOK TIME** 10 minutes · **TOTAL TIME** 20 minutes · **SERVES** 6

This dish was inspired by a version I had at a cute restaurant in Greenwich Village in New York called Palma—a sweet little spot that reminds me of an Italian garden. But their ravioli? It's incredible. Homemade cheese ravioli blanketed in their house-made cacio e pepe sauce: it's all about cheese and fresh cracked pepper. YUM! I created a much simpler version for busy nights at home. You can make homemade ravioli, pick up some packaged ones from your local grocery store, or, even better, grab some fresh from your favorite local Italian spot! It's the sauce that's important—and I like to finish mine with brown butter and fresh herbs for ultimate deliciousness.

Fine pink Himalayan salt

1 pound fresh cheese ravioli

1 tablespoon extra-virgin olive oil

3 garlic cloves, finely chopped or grated

2 teaspoons freshly ground black pepper

8 tablespoons (1 stick) salted butter

1 cup freshly grated Parmesan cheese

$\frac{1}{2}$ cup freshly grated pecorino cheese

2 tablespoons fresh thyme leaves

Chopped fresh basil, for serving

1. Bring a large pot of salted water to a boil over high heat. Add the ravioli and cook until al dente according to package directions. Reserve 1¼ cups pasta cooking water, then drain.

2. Heat the olive oil in a large skillet over medium heat. When the oil is shimmering, add a third of the garlic and the pepper and cook, stirring, until toasted, about 1 minute. Add 4 tablespoons of the butter. When melted, add the ravioli, 1 cup of the reserved pasta cooking water, the Parmesan, and pecorino. Toss vigorously to melt the cheese and create a creamy sauce, adding more pasta cooking water, if needed, to achieve the desired consistency. Season with salt.

3. Meanwhile, melt the remaining 4 tablespoons butter in a small skillet over medium heat. Cook until the butter is lightly browned, 3 to 4 minutes, then add the remaining garlic and cook for another 30 seconds, until fragrant. Remove from the heat and stir in the thyme.

4. Divide the ravioli among plates and spoon the garlic butter over each serving. Top with fresh basil and enjoy!

sun-dried tomato chicken carbonara

PREP TIME 20 minutes · **COOK TIME** 20 minutes · **TOTAL TIME** 40 minutes · **SERVES** 6

If you love chicken pasta *and* also enjoy a creamy pasta, this dish is the best of both worlds. Italian-seasoned chicken tossed with creamy carbonara sauce and sun-dried tomatoes, which I think are a real secret to deliciousness. They have the best flavor, no matter the season. The trick to a great carbonara is using room temperature ingredients and being sure you have everything ready to go before you start cooking the pasta. That means do ALL of the prep, then start cooking. I love to use long-cut pasta here, but you can use whatever you like. Just be sure you don't skimp on the cheese and the fresh basil on top!

6 slices thick-cut bacon, chopped

1 (8-ounce) jar oil-packed sun-dried tomatoes, chopped, plus 3 tablespoons of the the jarred oil

1 pound boneless, skinless chicken breasts, cubed

1 tablespoon Homemade Italian Seasoning (recipe follows) or store-bought Italian seasoning

Fine pink Himalayan salt and freshly ground black pepper

4 large egg yolks

$^1/_3$ cup heavy cream

$1^1/_2$ cups freshly grated Parmesan cheese, plus more for serving

1 pound pasta

$^1/_4$ cup chopped fresh basil

1. In a large skillet over medium-high heat, cook the bacon, stirring occasionally, until crisp, 5 to 7 minutes. Using a slotted spoon, transfer the bacon to a paper towel–lined plate. Drain off from the pan all but 1 tablespoon of the bacon fat.

2. Add the sun-dried tomato oil to the skillet and place over medium-high heat. Add the chicken, Italian seasoning, and salt and pepper. Cook, stirring occasionally, until the chicken is golden brown and opaque, about 5 minutes.

3. Meanwhile, in a small bowl, whisk together the egg yolks, cream, and Parmesan.

4. Bring a large pot of salted water to a boil. Add the pasta and cook until al dente according to package directions. Reserve 1 cup of pasta cooking water, then drain. Off the heat, return the pasta back to the hot pot.

5. Add the egg mixture to the pasta, tossing quickly to prevent the eggs from scrambling, and mixing until the pasta is nicely coated with sauce. If necessary, add the reserved pasta water, $^1/_3$ cup at a time, to thin the sauce to reach your desired consistency. Add the chicken, sun-dried tomatoes, and bacon and gently toss to combine. Stir in the basil to wilt, about 1 minute. Season with salt and pepper.

6. Finish with freshly grated Parmesan and a grind of black pepper.

homemade italian seasoning

—————— **MAKES ABOUT** $^1/_2$ **CUP** ——————

2 tablespoons dried basil

2 tablespoons dried oregano

2 teaspoons dried thyme

1 teaspoon dried rosemary

1 teaspoon dried sage

1 teaspoon garlic powder

1 teaspoon onion powder

In a lidded glass jar, combine the basil, oregano, thyme, rosemary, sage, garlic powder, and onion powder and stir to mix well. Store at room temperature in a cool, dark place for up to 6 months.

spicy skillet lasagna

PREP TIME 20 minutes · **COOK TIME** 35 minutes · **TOTAL TIME** 55 minutes, plus standing time · **SERVES** 6 to 8

I make lasagna a lot for my family, and even more so when I entertain. I think it's the perfect dish for guests because, if you need to, you can make two or even three to cater easily to what everyone likes to eat. I usually do a classic red-sauce lasagna, then a vegetarian white lasagna. If I am making a third, it might be butternut squash or something spicy! I love them all. This version is especially great when you are more crunched for time. My trick is mixing broken lasagna noodles or taccole pasta into the same skillet the base sauce is already in. I cook the noodles right in the sauce, then add cheese on top and bake away! It's super easy and results in a quick lasagna dinner with half the effort. Serve it with your favorite wine and bread on the side. Oh, and the Mean Green Salad (page 82) goes perfectly with it!

6 ounces spicy salami, chopped

½ pound 80/20 ground beef or ground chicken

1 medium yellow onion, chopped

4 garlic cloves, chopped

1 to 2 tablespoons Homemade Italian Seasoning (page 128) or store-bought Italian seasoning

2 tablespoons crushed Calabrian chile peppers

Fine pink Himalayan salt and freshly ground black pepper

Crushed red pepper flakes

1 pound taccole or broken lasagna noodles

1 bell pepper, any color, chopped

1 (14-ounce) can crushed San Marzano tomatoes

1 (24-ounce) jar marinara sauce (I like Rao's)

1½ cups shredded provolone cheese

1½ cups shredded mozzarella cheese

Chopped fresh basil, for serving

1. Preheat the oven to 425°F. Line a baking sheet with foil or parchment paper.

2. In a very large, oven-safe high-sided skillet over high heat, cook the salami until crisp, about 5 minutes. Add the ground beef and onion, and cook, breaking up the beef with a wooden spoon, until it begins to brown, about 5 minutes. Reduce the heat to medium, add the garlic, Italian seasoning, and Calabrian chile peppers, and season with salt and pepper and red pepper flakes. Cook, stirring, until fragrant, about 2 minutes.

3. Stir in the noodles and bell pepper, then add 3 cups of water. Bring to a simmer and cook until the noodles are tender but still have a bite, 5 to 8 minutes. Stir in the crushed tomatoes and 2 cups of the marinara sauce. Spoon the remaining sauce over the skillet. Top evenly with the provolone and mozzarella.

4. Place the skillet on the prepared baking sheet. Bake until the cheese is melted and bubbling, 15 to 20 minutes. Remove the lasagna from the oven and let stand for 10 minutes. Garnish with fresh basil and serve straight from the skillet.

vegetarian

chickpea curry
with hot harissa oil

PREP TIME 15 minutes · **COOK TIME** 30 minutes · **TOTAL TIME** 45 minutes · **SERVES** 6

This dish is simple, which is one of my favorite things about it, but the real specialness of this curry comes from the harissa oil. It's spicy with a touch of smokiness, and I think it adds a layer of interesting flavor that chickpea curry recipes can sometimes lack. This curry happens to be very saucy, so I serve it with buttery naan for optimal scooping. Spoons are optional!

4 tablespoons (½ stick) salted butter

1 medium yellow onion, chopped

1 (14-ounce) can chickpeas, drained and rinsed

4 medium carrots, chopped

2 tablespoons tomato paste

4 garlic cloves, chopped

1 (1-inch) piece fresh ginger, chopped or grated

1 tablespoon curry powder

2 teaspoons smoked paprika

Fine pink Himalayan salt and freshly ground black pepper

1 (14-ounce) can full-fat unsweetened coconut milk

⅓ cup harissa sauce

1½ cups chopped fresh baby spinach

2 tablespoons fresh lemon juice

Hot Harissa Oil

1½ tablespoons toasted sesame oil

1 tablespoon harissa sauce

2 tablespoons sesame seeds

Crushed red pepper flakes

Fine pink Himalayan salt

For Serving

Plain Greek yogurt

Fresh cilantro and/ or mint leaves

1. In a large Dutch oven set over medium heat, melt the butter. Add the onion and cook, stirring, until translucent and beginning to brown, about 5 minutes. Add the chickpeas, carrots, tomato paste, garlic, ginger, curry powder, and paprika. Season with salt and pepper. Cook, stirring occasionally, until very fragrant and the vegetables are beginning to soften, about 5 minutes.

2. Add the coconut milk and harissa. Increase the heat to high and bring to a boil, then reduce the heat to medium-low and simmer until the mixture has thickened, 20 to 30 minutes. Stir in the spinach and lemon juice. Taste and add salt and pepper as needed.

3. Meanwhile, make the hot harissa oil. In a small bowl, stir together the sesame oil, harissa, sesame seeds, and a pinch each of red pepper flakes and salt.

4. To serve, divide the curry among bowls. Add a dollop of yogurt and drizzle with the harissa oil, then top with fresh herbs.

mom's cheesy potato casserole

PREP TIME 30 minutes · **COOK TIME** 1 hour · **TOTAL TIME** 1 hour 30 minutes · **SERVES** 8

When we were growing up, everyone requested my mom's cheesy potatoes, which, as you might guess, were made with a few cans of Campbell's soup, plus so much sour cream, butter, and cheese. Some people call them funeral potatoes! For the longest time—and I am talking years—I tried to re-create her recipe without the canned goods, but nothing ever lived up to the classic. That is, until I started to get creative. This recipe is where I eventually landed, and my family agrees that these are just as good, if not better, than my mom's version. Sometimes I serve these as a side dish with the steak on page 205. Other times, they're the main course along with a big salad—I recommend the Mean Green Salad (page 82), and either the Roasted Broccoli Salad (page 85) or the Herby Double Tomato Salad (page 86). Then you're all set for a fun vegetarian dinner party!

2 pounds frozen shredded or diced hash-brown potatoes, thawed

8 tablespoons (1 stick) salted butter, melted, plus 2 tablespoons, at room temperature

2 cups shredded sharp cheddar cheese

$\frac{1}{2}$ cup freshly grated Parmesan cheese

2 cups sour cream

$\frac{1}{2}$ cup low-sodium vegetable broth

2 teaspoons vegan Worcestershire sauce

2 green onions, thinly sliced

1 tablespoon plus 1 teaspoon garlic powder

3 teaspoons onion powder

1 teaspoon sweet paprika

$\frac{1}{2}$ teaspoon cayenne pepper

Fine pink Himalayan salt and freshly ground black pepper

2 cups shredded Colby Jack cheese

2 cups cornflakes

Chopped fresh parsley and/or thyme, for serving

1. Preheat the oven to 375°F.

2. Place the potatoes in a 9 x 13-inch baking dish. If using diced potatoes, lightly mash with a fork, leaving them a bit chunky. Add the melted butter, cheddar, Parmesan, sour cream, vegetable broth, Worcestershire, green onions, 1 tablespoon of the garlic powder, 2 teaspoons of the onion powder, $\frac{1}{2}$ teaspoon of the paprika, and the cayenne. Season with salt and pepper. Mix well to coat evenly. Top with the Colby Jack.

3. In a medium bowl, combine the cornflakes, the 2 tablespoons room-temperature butter, the remaining 1 teaspoon garlic powder, 1 teaspoon onion powder, and $\frac{1}{2}$ teaspoon paprika. Stir to mix well. Sprinkle evenly over the potatoes.

4. Cover the baking dish with aluminum foil and bake until lightly bubbling, 35 to 40 minutes. Remove the foil and continue baking until the top is golden and crispy, 15 minutes more. Sprinkle with herbs and serve straight from the baking dish.

pan-fried veggie potstickers
with sweet chili ginger sauce

PREP TIME 15 minutes · **COOK TIME** 15 minutes · **TOTAL TIME** 30 minutes · **SERVES** 4 to 6

Everyone loves a good potsticker, but glazing these with brown butter makes them unique—and truly amazing. Once you make these, you will want to serve them every other week. That's how good they are! You can use store-bought frozen potstickers for a super-quick meal, but if you make the homemade version, do up a big batch and keep those in your freezer for future fast dinners. They are worth the effort, and they'll come in handy on busy weeknights!

Sweet Chili Ginger Sauce

1/2 cup tamari or
low-sodium soy sauce

2 to 3 tablespoons chili oil

2 tablespoons rice vinegar

2 tablespoons thinly sliced
pickled sushi ginger

1 tablespoon honey

1 tablespoon toasted
sesame seeds

Potstickers

Avocado oil, for pan-frying

30 to 40 Homemade Veggie
Potstickers (recipe follows)
or frozen store-bought
vegetable potstickers

4 tablespoons (1/2 stick)
salted butter

2 tablespoons tamari or
low-sodium soy sauce

3 green onions, thinly sliced

1. Make the sweet chili ginger sauce. In a medium bowl, combine the tamari, chili oil, vinegar, ginger, honey, and sesame seeds. Stir to mix well.

2. Cook the potstickers. Heat 2 tablespoons of avocado oil in a large skillet over medium heat. When the oil is shimmering, add as many potstickers as can fit comfortably in a single layer and cook until the bottoms begin to brown, about 30 seconds. Carefully add 1/2 cup water (it will splatter!), cover, and cook for about 3 minutes. Reduce the heat to medium-low and let the potstickers cook until the wrappers are translucent and the bottoms are nicely browned, 3 to 5 minutes more. Set the cooked potstickers aside and cover to keep warm. Repeat with the remaining potstickers, adding more oil as needed.

3. When all the potstickers have been cooked, wipe out the skillet and add the butter. Place over medium-high heat and arrange the potstickers in the pan, working in batches if necessary. Cook until the butter browns and the potstickers are crispy, 2 to 3 minutes. Remove the skillet from the heat, add the tamari, and toss to coat.

4. To serve, arrange the potstickers on a platter and top with green onions. Serve with the sweet chili ginger sauce alongside.

homemade veggie potstickers

2 tablespoons sesame oil

1 pound shiitake or cremini mushrooms

2 cups shredded mixed vegetables, such as carrots, cabbage, and/or zucchini

2 shallots, chopped

2 garlic cloves, finely chopped or grated

1 (1-inch) piece fresh ginger, chopped or grated

2 tablespoons tamari or low-sodium soy sauce

Freshly ground black pepper

30 to 40 round dumpling or wonton wrappers

Place a large skillet over medium-high heat and add the sesame oil. When the oil is shimmering, add the mushrooms, shredded vegetables, shallots, garlic, and ginger. Cook, stirring occasionally, until the mushrooms are tender, about 5 minutes. Add the tamari and a large pinch of pepper. Cook, stirring often, until the flavors are melded and the mushrooms begin to caramelize, 2 to 3 minutes more. Remove from the heat and transfer the contents of the skillet to a strainer placed over a bowl to let any excess liquid drain out. Let cool. To assemble, spoon about 1 tablespoon of drained filling into the middle of each wrapper. Lightly brush water around the edges, then fold the edges of the wrapper up around the filling, pinching in the center to seal. Repeat with the remaining filling and wrappers.

note: The potstickers can be cooked immediately or frozen. To freeze, arrange them on a parchment-lined baking sheet and freeze until firm, at least 30 minutes, then transfer to a zip-top bag and store in the freezer for up to 3 months.

whole roasted cauliflower
with garlic tahini & dates

PREP TIME 15 minutes · COOK TIME 55 minutes · TOTAL TIME 1 hour 10 minutes · SERVES 4

Something about the combination of a spice-rubbed cauliflower head with a creamy, garlicky sauce and sweet dates is amazing. The trick to this recipe is COVERING the cauliflower in garlic tahini sauce. It is THE most delicious way to enjoy roasted cauliflower. If I were you, I would make a big batch and keep this garlic tahini on hand. It is great on salads or to dress up any dish from grilled chicken to a plate full of roasted vegetables. You can even use it as a dip!

Fine pink Himalayan salt

1 large head cauliflower

1/2 cup extra-virgin olive oil

1 teaspoon smoked paprika

1 teaspoon chili powder

1 cup chopped mixed tender herbs, such as basil, dill, and/or cilantro

Crushed red pepper flakes

Freshly ground black pepper

1/2 cup medjool dates, pitted and torn (from about 5)

Garlic Tahini

1/2 cup tahini

2 garlic cloves, finely chopped or grated

Juice of 1 lemon

Fine pink Himalayan salt

1. Preheat the oven to 450°F.

2. Bring a large pot of salted water to a boil over high heat. Carefully add the cauliflower upside down, submerging it completely. Cook until knife-tender, about 7 minutes. Drain the cauliflower and set it on a towel, stem-side down, to dry for 5 to 10 minutes.

3. Place the cauliflower in a baking dish or oven-safe skillet and pour over 1/4 cup of the olive oil, covering the entire head. Season generously with salt. Bake until golden all over, about 45 minutes.

4. Meanwhile, in a small bowl, combine the remaining 1/4 cup olive oil, the paprika, chili powder, herbs, and red pepper flakes. Season with salt and pepper and stir to mix well.

5. Make the garlic tahini. In a spouted measuring cup, combine 1/3 cup of ice water, the tahini, garlic, and lemon juice. Season with salt and whisk until smooth, adding more water as needed to reach your desired consistency. Taste and add more salt as needed.

6. To serve, cut the cauliflower into wedges and arrange on a serving plate. Spoon the herby oil over the cauliflower, rubbing it in a bit. Pour over the garlic tahini to cover the cauliflower and scatter the dates on top. Serve warm.

tomato cheddar basil beans

PREP TIME 10 minutes · **COOK TIME** 20 minutes · **TOTAL TIME** 30 minutes · **SERVES** 4 to 6

During the summer, my mom makes tomato-cheddar toast for lunch all the time. She'll take sourdough bread, spread each piece with butter, then top it with cheddar cheese and a fresh tomato slice. She broils the toast until the cheese is super melty and bubbly and finishes it with a sprinkle of fresh basil on top. She calls it "bubbled-up tomato cheddar toast." It is honestly so good! I took those flavors plus my recipe for a creamy tomato soup and created these very cheesy, very delicious beans. What could be better than a skillet full of cozy beans and cheese? Nothing! Be sure to serve these with toasted crusty bread to complete the experience.

¼ cup extra-virgin olive oil

1 shallot, finely chopped

4 garlic cloves, finely chopped or grated

1 teaspoon dried oregano

1 (6-ounce) can tomato paste

1 to 2 teaspoons crushed red pepper flakes

½ cup heavy cream

½ cup basil pesto

Fine pink Himalayan salt and freshly ground black pepper

3 (15-ounce) cans white beans, such as butter, cannellini, or navy, drained

1 cup shredded cheddar cheese

¼ cup fresh basil, roughly chopped, plus more for serving

½ cup shredded mozzarella cheese

Crusty bread, for serving

1. Preheat the broiler.

2. In a large skillet over medium heat, heat the olive oil. When the oil is shimmering, add the shallot and cook until it begins to soften, 1 minute. Add the garlic and oregano and cook, stirring, until fragrant, about 2 minutes more.

3. Reduce the heat to low, add the tomato paste and red pepper flakes, and cook, stirring, until the tomato paste darkens to a rich brick red, about 4 minutes. Stir in 1 cup of water, then the cream and pesto. Season with salt and pepper. Add the beans and ½ cup of the cheddar, tossing until the cheese melts. Simmer, stirring occasionally, until the beans are well coated and the flavors are melded, about 10 minutes. Stir in the basil and cook just to wilt, one minute more. Taste and add more salt and pepper as needed.

4. Top with the remaining ½ cup cheddar and the mozzarella. Broil until the cheese is melted and bubbling, about 2 minutes.

5. Divide the beans among bowls and top with more basil. Serve with bread alongside for scooping and dipping.

black bean quesadillas
with creamy jalapeño sauce

PREP TIME 15 minutes · COOK TIME 15 minutes · TOTAL TIME 30 minutes · SERVES 4

I will always love making quesadillas. They are one of the first foods I made when I started to cook for my family. I used to do chicken, rice, and cheese quesadillas for my brothers all the time back when I was in high school—and they still request those same quesadillas! But this is my vegetarian variation, and some people love these even more! The jalapeño sauce is what makes them so special. I love to use it in the quesadilla and then on top for serving. Don't forget those fresh chunks of avocado, too. YUM!

Creamy Jalapeño Sauce

½ cup plain Greek yogurt or sour cream

¼ cup mayonnaise

2 tablespoons fresh lime juice

1 jalapeño, seeded if desired, roughly chopped

1 cup fresh cilantro

¼ cup chopped green onions

1 teaspoon garlic powder

Fine pink Himalayan salt

Quesadillas

1 (15-ounce) can black beans, drained

¾ cup red enchilada sauce

1 small yellow onion, chopped

1 to 2 chipotle peppers in adobo, finely chopped

1 teaspoon dried oregano

Fine pink Himalayan salt and freshly ground black pepper

1 cup shredded pepper Jack cheese

1 cup shredded Monterey Jack cheese

4 to 6 flour tortillas

1 cup chopped fresh cilantro, plus more for serving

Extra-virgin olive oil

1 avocado, diced

1. Make the creamy jalapeño sauce. In a blender or food processor, combine the yogurt, mayo, lime juice, jalapeño, cilantro, green onions, and garlic powder. Season with salt. Blend on high until completely smooth, 1 to 2 minutes. Taste and add more salt as needed.

2. Make the quesadillas. In a large skillet set over medium heat, combine the beans, enchilada sauce, onion, chipotle peppers, and oregano. Season with salt and pepper. Cook, stirring occasionally, until the onion is soft and the sauce thickens around the beans, about 10 minutes. Remove the skillet from the heat.

3. To assemble, in a small bowl, toss together the pepper Jack and Monterey Jack. Set aside and reserve about ½ cup. With the tortillas arranged on a work surface, evenly layer onto one half of each: the cheese mixture, saucy beans, and cilantro. Sprinkle the reserved cheese on top, then fold the tortillas over to enclose the filling.

4. In a large skillet over medium heat, add a drizzle of olive oil. When the oil is shimmering, add the quesadillas, in batches, and cook, turning once, until the outside is crisp and golden and the cheese is melting, 2 to 3 minutes per side.

5. Serve the quesadillas hot, topped with the creamy jalapeño sauce, avocado, and more cilantro.

cheesy stuffed spaghetti squash
with garlic basil butter

PREP TIME 20 minutes · **COOK TIME** 1 hour · **TOTAL TIME** 1 hour 20 minutes · **SERVES** 4 to 6

I think this is probably my mom's favorite recipe, but, surprisingly, I have managed to turn my entire family into spaghetti squash people. I make this dish a lot throughout the fall and winter, when spaghetti squash is at its tastiest. While it's a delicious meal on its own, I also love to pair it with steaks, especially when my brothers are at the dinner table. The garlic butter topping on each squash is essential—do not skip it. When you dig your fork into each spaghetti boat, swirl the butter around to coat all the creamy strands of squash.

1¼ cups whole milk
or heavy cream

4 ounces cream cheese, melted

2 cups chopped Tuscan kale

1 cup freshly grated
Parmesan cheese

1 shallot, chopped

1 teaspoon dried oregano

Fine pink Himalayan salt and
freshly ground black pepper

Crushed red pepper flakes

2 medium (3-pound) spaghetti
squash, halved through the
stem end and seeds removed

8 garlic cloves, skin on

1 cup shredded
provolone cheese

½ cup loosely packed
fresh basil, chopped

4 tablespoons (½ stick) salted
butter, at room temperature

1 to 2 tablespoons
toasted pine nuts

1 teaspoon honey

1. Preheat the oven to 425°F.

2. In a medium bowl, combine the milk, cream cheese, kale, Parmesan, shallot, and oregano and stir to mix well. Season with salt, black pepper, and red pepper flakes.

3. Place the squash on a baking sheet and season the cut sides with salt and pepper. Divide the cream cheese mixture evenly among the squash cavities. Arrange the whole garlic cloves around the squash halves on the baking sheet.

4. Cover the squash (not the garlic) loosely with aluminum foil and bake until they are very tender, 45 minutes to 1 hour, watching to make sure the garlic does not burn. Remove the pan from the oven and set aside the garlic cloves. Sprinkle equal portions of the provolone over the squash. Return to the oven and bake uncovered until the cheese is melted, 12 to 15 minutes.

5. Peel and chop the roasted garlic and transfer it to a small bowl. Add the basil, butter, pine nuts, and honey, and stir to mix well. To serve, spread the garlic basil butter over the baked squash, then use a fork to scrape the squash into strands, mixing the cheese and butter into them.

roasted butternut squash unstuffed manicotti

PREP TIME 40 minutes · **COOK TIME** 1 hour 5 minutes · **TOTAL TIME** 1 hour 45 minutes · **SERVES** 6 to 8

The lasagna recipe my aunt Katie shared with my mom so many years ago is the recipe I use, too—a white spinach version that can be made with or without chicken. That white sauce is Aunt Katie's secret. She would make a double batch to ensure her lasagna was smothered and never dry. In fact, her sauce is so good that I use it as the base for most of my white pastas! In this dish, I combined it with creamy roasted butternut squash puree—such a wonderful combination in the fall! But who wants to fuss around with stuffing manicotti shells? Instead, I layer the pasta tubes with the other ingredients, and everything melts right into them—they basically stuff themselves while baking! It works like magic and saves so much time. This dish is pretty on any dinner table and is a great vegetarian option for dinner parties.

1 tablespoon extra-virgin olive oil

2 cups cubed butternut squash

6 garlic cloves

2 tablespoons fresh thyme leaves

1 tablespoon chopped fresh rosemary

1 teaspoon smoked paprika

1 teaspoon chipotle chile powder

Fine pink Himalayan salt and freshly ground black pepper

1 pound manicotti shells

8 tablespoons (1 stick) salted butter, plus more for greasing

2 tablespoons chopped fresh sage

1/2 cup all-purpose flour

2 cups milk of your choice

2 cups dry white wine, such as pinot grigio or sauvignon blanc, or low-sodium vegetable broth

1 cup shredded mozzarella cheese

1/2 cup freshly grated Parmesan cheese

1 cup whole-milk ricotta cheese

2 cups shredded provolone cheese

2 (10-ounce) packages frozen spinach, thawed, drained, and squeezed dry

1. Place a rack in the top third of the oven and preheat to 400°F.

2. In a 9 x 13-inch baking dish, toss together the olive oil, squash, garlic, thyme, rosemary, paprika, and chipotle chile powder. Season with salt and pepper. Bake until the squash is tender, 25 to 30 minutes.

3. Meanwhile, bring a large pot of salted water to a boil over high heat. Add the pasta and cook until al dente according to package directions, then drain and set aside.

4. While the squash and pasta cook, make the cheese sauce. In a medium pan over medium heat, melt together the butter and sage and cook until fragrant, 2 to 3 minutes. Whisk in the flour and cook, stirring, until lightly colored, about 1 minute. Add the milk and wine, whisking until smooth. Increase the heat to high and bring to a boil. Cook until thickened, 1 to 2 minutes. Remove from the heat and add 1/2 cup of the mozzarella and the Parmesan, stirring until completely melted and the sauce is smooth.

5. Transfer the roasted butternut squash mixture to a food processor and add the ricotta. Puree until smooth, scraping down the sides as needed, about 1 minute. Add the provolone and spinach and puree until broken down and well incorporated, scraping down the sides as needed, about 2 minutes. Taste and add salt and pepper as needed.

6. Wipe out the baking dish from the squash, then lightly grease it. Spread a third of the cheese sauce over the bottom. Arrange the manicotti shells in an even layer on top of the sauce. Add the squash puree, covering the manicotti. Sprinkle over the remaining 1/2 cup mozzarella and pour the remaining cheese sauce over the top.

7. Cover loosely with aluminum foil and bake for about 20 minutes, then remove the foil and bake until the sauce is bubbling, 15 to 20 minutes. Turn on the broiler and cook, watching closely, until the cheese is just beginning to brown, about 1 minute. Serve from the baking dish.

lemon pesto orzo
with buttery walnuts & kale

PREP TIME 15 minutes · **COOK TIME** 25 minutes · **TOTAL TIME** 40 minutes · **SERVES** 4

When I started making this orzo dish a few summers ago, it was a variation on my mom's "souper" rice, which, if you've been here for a while, you know she would often make us for lunch. It's essentially rice with a bit of chicken broth (yup, she used a can of Campbell's soup). It only took a few minutes to make and was very yummy. My version is a bit more elevated, and, well, it's definitely WAY more delicious. (Sorry, Mom!) The walnuts really steal the show here. They are the perfect spicy, sweet CRUNCH atop this creamy bowl of orzo. Make this dish when your spring and summer garden or farmers' market is bursting with kale and basil.

Buttery Walnuts

1 cup raw walnuts, chopped

1 tablespoon chopped fresh rosemary

1 teaspoon light brown sugar

1/2 teaspoon cayenne pepper

Fine pink Himalayan salt

3 tablespoons salted butter, sliced

Orzo

3 tablespoons salted butter

1 garlic clove, chopped

1 tablespoon lemon zest

Freshly ground black pepper

1 pound orzo

4 cups low-sodium vegetable broth, plus more as needed

1 bunch kale, stemmed and torn

1 cup freshly grated Parmesan cheese

1/2 cup basil pesto

Torn fresh basil, for serving

1. Make the walnuts. Preheat the oven to 400°F. Line a baking sheet with parchment paper.

2. On the prepared baking sheet, toss together the walnuts, rosemary, brown sugar, cayenne, and a pinch of salt. Spread in an even layer and scatter the butter over them. Bake until the butter melts, about 3 minutes, then toss to coat. Bake, watching closely and stirring once or twice, until the nuts are toasted and the sugar has melted, 4 to 5 minutes more.

3. Meanwhile, make the orzo. Melt the butter in a large Dutch oven over medium heat. Add the garlic and lemon zest and season with pepper. Cook, stirring, until the garlic is fragrant, about 1 minute. Stir in the orzo and cook, stirring several times, until the orzo is well coated with butter and lightly toasted, about 2 minutes. Add the broth, then increase the heat to high and bring to a boil. Reduce the heat to low and simmer, stirring often, until the orzo is al dente, 10 to 12 minutes. If the broth has been absorbed and the orzo isn't done, add more as needed (or use water) and continue cooking and stirring until done.

4. Stir in the kale and Parmesan and cook until warmed through, about 2 minutes. As the orzo thickens, add more broth or water as needed to thin; it should have a creamy consistency. Remove the pot from the heat. Gently swirl the pesto into the orzo, stopping short of fully mixing it.

5. To serve, divide the orzo among bowls and top with the buttery walnuts and fresh basil.

curried lentils
with spicy sesame butter

PREP TIME 15 minutes · COOK TIME 45 minutes · TOTAL TIME 1 hour · SERVES 6

During the fall and winter, I make curry at least once a week. Most of the time I'll make my butter chicken or a quick Thai red curry. But whenever my cousins are in town, I often make lentil and bean curries—unlike my brothers, they love legumes, so it's always so fun to cook for them! This dish is fast, since lentils cook up way quicker than dried beans—just about 20 minutes, no soaking required. I use a mix of Thai red curry paste and Indian garam masala to make it super flavorful. I love the marriage of their spicy and warm flavors.

Curried Lentils

2 tablespoons ghee
or salted butter

1 small yellow onion, chopped

1 shallot, chopped

2 garlic cloves, chopped

1 (1-inch) piece fresh ginger,
chopped or grated

1 tablespoon garam masala

1 teaspoon ground turmeric

1 (6-ounce) can tomato paste

2 tablespoons Thai
red curry paste

4 cups low-sodium
vegetable broth or water,
plus more as needed

2 cups green or black lentils

2 medium sweet
potatoes, cubed

Fine pink Himalayan salt

1 (14-ounce) can full-fat
unsweetened coconut milk

1/3 cup fresh cilantro, chopped

Spicy Sesame Butter

6 tablespoons ghee
or salted butter

2 tablespoons sesame seeds

1 to 2 teaspoons crushed
red pepper flakes

1/2 teaspoon smoked paprika

For Serving

Cooked jasmine rice

Chopped fresh cilantro

Plain Greek yogurt

Naan

1. Make the curried lentils. Melt the ghee in a large Dutch oven over medium heat. Add the onion, shallot, garlic, and ginger and cook, stirring, until fragrant and beginning to brown, 4 to 5 minutes. Add the garam masala and turmeric and cook, stirring, until toasted, about 1 minute. Stir in the tomato paste and curry paste and cook until darkened in color, 2 to 3 minutes. Add the broth and use a wooden spoon to scrape up any browned bits from the bottom of the pan.

2. Add the lentils and sweet potatoes and season generously with salt. Increase the heat to high and bring to a boil, then reduce the heat to low. Cook, stirring occasionally, until the lentils and sweet potatoes are tender, 20 to 25 minutes, adding more liquid as needed to keep a saucy consistency.

3. Stir in the coconut milk and cook until the flavors are nicely melded, 8 to 10 minutes more. Stir in the cilantro.

4. Meanwhile, make the sesame butter. In a small skillet over medium heat, combine the ghee, sesame seeds, red pepper flakes, and paprika. Cook, stirring frequently, just until the butter begins to brown, 3 to 4 minutes. Remove from the heat.

5. To serve, spoon the lentils over bowls of rice and top with drizzles of spicy sesame butter. Sprinkle with cilantro and serve with yogurt and naan.

all-the-toppings sandwich
with spicy mayo

PREP TIME 15 minutes · COOK TIME 5 minutes · TOTAL TIME 20 minutes · MAKES 2 sandwiches

My brother Red loves a good sandwich. He is always down to try a new combination, and he especially loves when there's spicy mayo involved. He was telling me about a sandwich he had once, layered with roasted peppers, multiple kinds of pickles, and sun-dried tomatoes. It sounded so good, I had to ask him to give me more details! Basically, this is a heavily layered and stuffed grilled cheese with SO many briny, pickled things. If I can find it, I love to make this one with sourdough bread studded with olives or a great rye. And don't forget the chips on the side—Red wouldn't have it any other way!

Spicy Mayo

1/2 cup mayonnaise

2 tablespoons crushed Calabrian chile peppers in oil

1 to 2 tablespoons pickle or pepperoncini brine

1 teaspoon hot sauce (I like Frank's RedHot)

1 teaspoon smoked paprika

1/4 teaspoon chipotle chile powder

Fine pink Himalayan salt

Sandwiches

4 slices rye or sourdough bread, toasted

1 tablespoon salted butter, at room temperature

1/3 cup basil pesto

4 to 6 slices Gouda and/or Havarti cheese

2 roasted bell peppers, sliced

1/3 cup sun-dried tomatoes, sliced

1/3 cup sliced dill pickles

1/3 cup chopped pepperoncini

1/3 cup pitted mixed olives, chopped

2 cups baby arugula

1 avocado, sliced

Pickled Red Onions (recipe follows)

1. Make the spicy mayo. In a small bowl, combine the mayo, Calabrian peppers, brine, hot sauce, paprika, chipotle chile powder, and salt. Mix well to combine. Taste and adjust the seasonings as needed.

2. Make the sandwiches. Turn the broiler to high.

3. Working on a baking sheet, lightly butter one side of each piece of toast. Flip over and spread the other sides of all four slices with some of the spicy mayo, then the pesto. Layer the cheese over the pesto. Broil for 3 to 4 minutes until the cheese is melty and bubbling.

4. On two of the pieces of bread, layer on the roasted peppers, sun-dried tomatoes, pickles, pepperoncini, olives, arugula, avocado, and red onions. Add the top slices of bread, cheesy sides down. Cut the sandwiches in half and serve warm with the extra mayo alongside for dipping.

pickled red onions

— MAKES ABOUT 1/2 CUP —

1 medium red onion, very thinly sliced

1/2 cup apple cider vinegar or white vinegar

2 teaspoons fine pink Himalayan salt

1 teaspoon honey

Pack the onions tightly into a glass jar with a lid (an 8-ounce mason jar is a good choice), leaving about 1/2-inch space at the top. In a small pot set over high heat, bring the vinegar, salt, honey, and 1/2 cup water to a boil, stirring until the salt dissolves. Remove the pot from the heat and pour the mixture over the onions. Seal the jar and let cool to room temperature. Use immediately, or store, sealed and refrigerated, for up to 1 month. The longer the onions sit, the more flavor they will develop.

spicy miso-coconut broth noodles
with sesame crunch

PREP TIME 15 minutes · COOK TIME 15 minutes · TOTAL TIME 30 minutes · SERVES 4

Asher loves soup, noodles, and any dish with soy sauce. She is a salt-and-starch girl through and through. This dish has become one of her favorites. Sometimes I add shredded chicken if my brothers are eating dinner with us, too, but she and I both love these noodles as is, with the mushrooms and spinach. I usually add soft eggs on top, which is always a yummy touch! But Asher says no matter what, you have to use ramen noodles when you make this. They're always more delicious—and she's not wrong!

2 tablespoons ghee or salted butter

1½ cups sliced shiitake mushrooms

6 garlic cloves, chopped

2 medium shallots, chopped

1 (1-inch) piece fresh ginger, chopped or grated

Crushed red pepper flakes

6 cups low-sodium vegetable broth

1 (14-ounce) can full-fat unsweetened coconut milk

¼ cup tamari or low-sodium soy sauce

¼ cup white miso paste

2 to 4 tablespoons chili paste, to taste (I like gochujang or Thai red curry paste)

1 pound cooked ramen noodles, Chinese-style egg noodles, or rice noodles

2 cups fresh baby spinach, chopped

1 tablespoon toasted sesame oil, plus more for serving

Thinly sliced green onions, for serving

Sesame Crunch

1 tablespoon ghee or salted butter

½ cup panko breadcrumbs

⅓ cup sesame seeds

2 garlic cloves, finely chopped or grated

2 toasted nori sheets, crumbled

Fine pink Himalayan salt

1. Melt the ghee in a Dutch oven over medium-high heat. Add the mushrooms, garlic, shallots, and ginger and season with red pepper flakes. Cook, stirring, until the ingredients are fragrant and beginning to soften, about 2 minutes. Pour in the broth, coconut milk, and tamari, then add the miso and chili paste, whisking until smooth. Reduce the heat to low and simmer, stirring occasionally, until the flavors are melded, about 10 minutes. Stir in the noodles, spinach, and toasted sesame oil and cook until the noodles are hot and the spinach wilted, 1 to 2 minutes more.

2. Meanwhile, make the sesame crunch. Melt the ghee in a small skillet over medium-high heat. Add the panko, sesame seeds, and garlic and cook, stirring frequently, until lightly toasted, 3 to 4 minutes. Remove the skillet from the heat. Stir in the nori and season with salt.

3. To serve, ladle the broth and noodles into bowls. Spoon the sesame crunch over the top and finish with green onions and additional sesame oil.

note: If you have leftovers, you might want to store the noodles and broth separately–the noodles will absorb more liquid the longer they sit in it.

mushroom "carnitas" tacos
with creamy verde sauce

PREP TIME 15 minutes · **COOK TIME** 15 minutes · **TOTAL TIME** 30 minutes · **SERVES** 4

I know calling this dish "carnitas" is a stretch, but the braised-then-caramelized mushrooms really do take on a rich flavor and texture that feels similar to shredded pork. So we're going with it! I adore the mushrooms in these tacos, as do my dad and my friends. I have been making these for years, and my cousins always request them when they come to see us in Colorado! The key to achieving the best flavor is using a mix of mushrooms. I love baby bella (aka cremini) and shiitake, but you can definitely just use one or the other. The creamy verde sauce on top is a must-make for serving, too. You can't do tacos without a great salsa!

2 tablespoons salted butter

2 tablespoons extra-virgin olive oil

2 pounds sliced, mixed mushrooms, such as cremini and/or shiitake

1 tablespoon maple syrup

2 teaspoons chili powder

1 teaspoon smoked paprika

1 teaspoon ground cumin

1 teaspoon dried oregano

1 teaspoon garlic powder

1 tablespoon vegan Worcestershire sauce

Fine pink Himalayan salt and freshly ground black pepper

1 cup crumbled cotija cheese

1/2 cup chopped fresh cilantro

4 green onions, thinly sliced

2 tablespoons fresh lime juice

2 avocados, mashed

8 flour tortillas

Creamy Verde Sauce

3/4 cup salsa verde

1/2 cup sour cream or plain Greek yogurt

1 to 3 tablespoons pickled jalapeños, chopped

1. In a large skillet over high heat, melt the butter and olive oil together. Add the mushrooms and cook, stirring occasionally, until the mushrooms begin to caramelize, 8 to 10 minutes. Add the maple syrup, chili powder, paprika, cumin, oregano, and garlic powder and cook, stirring, until fragrant, about 1 minute. Add the Worcestershire sauce and cook until deeply caramelized, 2 minutes more. Season generously with salt and pepper and remove from the heat.

2. Meanwhile, in a small bowl, stir together the cotija, cilantro, green onions, and lime juice.

3. Make the creamy verde sauce. In a small bowl, stir together the salsa verde and sour cream until well combined. Stir in the jalapeños to taste.

4. Divide the mashed avocado evenly among the tortillas, spreading it all the way to the edges. (If you'd like to toast the tortillas before filling them, see the Note on page 38.) Top with the mushrooms, then the creamy verde sauce and cotija mixture.

chicken & pork

creamy green chile chicken enchiladas

PREP TIME 25 minutes · **COOK TIME** 20 minutes · **TOTAL TIME** 45 minutes, plus cooling time · **SERVES** 4 to 6

Classic beef enchiladas are delicious, and it's a dish I always enjoy making. But sometimes I like to switch it up and make green chile enchiladas with salsa verde. My version is not traditional, but these enchiladas are always popular and frequently requested by my family. To balance all the herby cilantro in the dish, I top the enchiladas with lots of yogurt, avocado slices, and then fresh basil to mix it up a little bit. I love the subtle flavor it adds!

4 ounces cream cheese, at room temperature

¾ cup milk of choice

1 (12- to 14-ounce) jar green chile enchilada sauce

1½ cups cooked shredded chicken

2 teaspoons onion powder

2 teaspoons ground cumin

1 teaspoon garlic powder

1 teaspoon chili powder

2 (4-ounce) cans diced green chiles

1 (10-ounce) bag frozen corn, thawed

1 cup shredded cheddar cheese

Fine pink Himalayan salt

12 corn or flour tortillas, warmed until pliable

2 cups shredded pepper Jack cheese

For Serving

Plain Greek yogurt or sour cream

Diced avocado

Sliced green onions

Crumbled cotija cheese

Thinly sliced fresh basil

Fresh lime juice

1. Preheat the oven to 400°F.

2. Place the cream cheese in a large spouted measuring cup. Slowly whisk in the milk until the cream cheese is smooth, then add half the jar of enchilada sauce.

3. In a large bowl, combine the chicken, onion powder, cumin, garlic powder, chili powder, green chiles, corn, and cheddar. Season with salt and stir to mix well. Add about a third of the cream cheese sauce and toss to coat.

4. To assemble, coat the bottom of a 9 x 13-inch baking dish with a few spoonfuls of the remaining enchilada sauce. Working with one tortilla at a time, spoon the chicken mixture down the center, roll it up, and place the filled tortillas in the baking dish, seam-side down. Repeat with the remaining tortillas and chicken mixture.

5. Pour the remaining cream sauce over the enchiladas, then the remaining enchilada sauce. Scatter the pepper Jack cheese over the top.

6. Bake the enchiladas until the cheese has melted and the sauce is bubbling, about 20 minutes. Let cool for about 10 minutes, then serve the enchiladas garnished with the toppings of your choice.

spicy chicken paprikash

PREP TIME 15 minutes · **COOK TIME** 30 minutes · **TOTAL TIME** 45 minutes · **SERVES** 6

I don't know why, but I hesitated to cook this dish for a long time. Now that I have, I love it! I make my sauce with two kinds of paprika (smoked and sweet), plus a touch of cayenne for some heat— it's really flavorful this way. And you have to use real, full-fat sour cream. It gives the sauce the best flavor and creaminess. The best part? It's all made in one skillet! My special touch comes when serving, though: soft pretzels, ideally homemade, but from the bakery or frozen is fine, too. That special crust flavor is perfect when dipped into the paprika sauce!

2 pounds boneless, skinless chicken thighs or breasts

Fine pink Himalayan salt and freshly ground black pepper

2 tablespoons extra-virgin olive oil

4 tablespoons ($\frac{1}{2}$ stick) salted butter

2 tablespoons all-purpose flour

1 large yellow onion, chopped

3 garlic cloves, chopped

2 tablespoons smoked paprika

1 tablespoon sweet paprika

1 teaspoon cayenne pepper

$\frac{1}{3}$ cup tomato paste

$\frac{3}{4}$ cup sour cream, at room temperature

Soft pretzels, for serving (optional)

1. Season the chicken all over with salt and pepper. In a large skillet over medium-high heat, heat the olive oil. When the oil is shimmering, add the chicken and cook, turning once, until it is golden brown, about 4 minutes per side. Transfer the chicken to a plate.

2. To the same skillet over medium heat, add 3 tablespoons of the butter, the flour, and the onion. Cook, stirring, until the onion is soft and just beginning to brown, about 5 minutes. Add the garlic, smoked paprika, sweet paprika, and cayenne and cook, stirring, until very fragrant, about 30 seconds. Add the tomato paste and cook, stirring, 1 minute more. Add 2 cups of water, stirring to form a sauce.

3. Return the chicken to the skillet, along with any collected juices. Reduce the heat to low, cover, and simmer gently until the meat is cooked through, 8 to 10 minutes. Stir in the sour cream and the remaining 1 tablespoon butter to incorporate. Taste and add more salt and pepper as needed.

4. Serve family style.

one-pot spiced chicken & dumplings

PREP TIME 25 minutes · **COOK TIME** 1 hour · **TOTAL TIME** 1 hour 25 minutes · **SERVES** 4 to 6

I used to make a classic version of chicken and dumplings a lot. That's the recipe on my website, and everyone seems to really enjoy it—everyone, that is, except my dad. He says it just doesn't have enough flavor for his taste buds! So one night while making my usual recipe, I changed it around a bit. I added some salsa verde I had in the fridge, then some sharp cheddar cheese. I knew it would be different, but I thought the creamy base would be great with the addition of some spice and cheese. Now this is one of my dad's favorite meals! He says the salsa swirled through really adds the best flavor! And bacon on top, too, because why not, right?

6 slices thick-cut bacon, chopped

1¾ cups all-purpose flour

1 cup chopped celery (from 2 stalks)

2 poblano peppers, seeded and chopped

2 shallots, thinly sliced

2 tablespoons fresh thyme leaves

Fine pink Himalayan salt and freshly ground black pepper

1 pound boneless, skinless chicken thighs or breasts

6 cups low-sodium chicken broth, plus more as needed

2 cups milk of your choice

¾ cup salsa verde

2 teaspoons baking powder

1 tablespoon chopped fresh sage, plus fresh sage leaves for serving

1 cup shredded white cheddar cheese

Thinly sliced green onion, for serving

1. In a large Dutch oven over medium heat, cook the bacon, stirring occasionally, until it is crisp and the fat has rendered, 5 to 6 minutes. Using a slotted spoon, transfer the bacon to a paper towel–lined plate. Drain off all but 1 tablespoon of the fat.

2. With the Dutch oven still over medium heat, stir in ¼ cup of the flour until smooth, then add the celery, poblanos, shallots, and thyme. Season with salt and pepper. Cook, stirring, until the flour is incorporated and the vegetables begin to soften, 4 to 5 minutes. Add the chicken, broth, 1 cup of the milk, and the salsa verde. Season with salt and pepper. Increase the heat to high and bring to a boil, then reduce the heat to medium-low and simmer until the chicken is cooked through, 18 to 20 minutes, adding more broth if needed. Transfer the chicken to a cutting board and use two forks to shred it into pieces.

3. Meanwhile, in a medium bowl, whisk together the remaining 1½ cups flour, the baking powder, sage, and a pinch each of salt and pepper. Add the remaining 1 cup milk and stir until just combined—do not overmix.

4. Stir the cheddar into the pot. Increase the heat to medium and bring the mixture to a gentle boil. Working quickly, drop in heaping tablespoons of the dough to form the dumplings. Cover and cook until the dumplings are puffy and cooked through, 10 to 12 minutes.

5. Return the shredded chicken to the pot. Taste and add salt and pepper as needed.

6. Divide the stew and dumplings among bowls and serve topped with crispy bacon, sage, and green onions.

baked chicken parm sandwich

PREP TIME 30 minutes · **COOK TIME** 20 minutes · **TOTAL TIME** 50 minutes · **SERVES** 4

I love a lot of recipes in this cookbook, but this sandwich is something special. It's a hard-core chicken Parm sandwich: toasted ciabatta with marinara and Parmesan, then crispy chicken cutlets, more, more cheese, a layer of crispy prosciutto, plus lots of fresh basil. Be sure you use a fresh loaf of ciabatta (I love the Whole Foods brand), your favorite marinara sauce, and good-quality mozzarella. Plus lots of freshly grated Parmesan—the pre-shredded stuff does not cut it here. We are not messing around! I took notes from all my brothers AND consulted our uncle Joe. Everyone has given this chicken Parm a ten out of ten. You just can't beat it.

Extra-virgin olive oil

8 to 12 thin slices of prosciutto

¾ cup all-purpose flour

3 large eggs

2 cups panko breadcrumbs

2 cups freshly grated Parmesan cheese

1 tablespoon Homemade Seasoned Salt (page 56) or store-bought seasoned salt

Fine pink Himalayan salt and freshly ground black pepper

4 to 6 chicken cutlets, or 3 boneless, skinless chicken breasts, halved horizontally

1 loaf ciabatta bread, halved lengthwise

1 large garlic clove, halved

1 cup marinara sauce (I like Rao's)

1 to 3 tablespoons crushed Calabrian chile peppers or crushed red pepper flakes

4 slices low-moisture whole-milk mozzarella cheese

4 slices provolone cheese

⅓ cup pepperoncini

1 to 2 cups loosely packed fresh basil leaves

1. Preheat the oven to 425°F.

2. Place a large skillet over medium-high heat and add 2 tablespoons of olive oil. When the oil is shimmering, add the prosciutto and cook, stirring occasionally, until crisp, about 5 minutes. Transfer the prosciutto to a plate.

3. Place the flour in a shallow dish. In a separate shallow dish, beat the eggs. In a third shallow dish, combine the panko, 1 cup of the Parmesan, the seasoned salt, and pepper. Line up the dishes in this order.

4. Dredge the chicken through the flour, turning to coat. Then dip it into the eggs, allowing excess to drip off. Lastly, place the chicken in the panko mixture, turning to coat both sides and gently pressing the mixture into place. Transfer the coated pieces to a plate.

5. Heat half an inch of olive oil in a large skillet over medium-high. When the oil is shimmering, add the chicken, in batches as necessary, and cook until golden brown on the bottom, 3 to 4 minutes. Flip the chicken and cook until golden brown all over, 3 to 4 minutes more. Transfer to a wire rack and season with pink salt.

6. Meanwhile, arrange the ciabatta cut-side up on a baking sheet. Drizzle each half with olive oil, then rub with the cut sides of the garlic. Bake until toasted, 3 to 5 minutes.

7. Spread the marinara on the bottom half of the ciabatta, then slather on the Calabrian chiles. In this order, layer with the mozzarella, the remaining 1 cup Parmesan, the chicken, provolone, and the prosciutto.

8. Bake the open sandwich until the cheese is melted and lightly bubbling, 8 to 10 minutes. Top with the pepperoncini and basil, then finish with the top half of the bread. Slice and serve immediately.

spicy thai basil chicken fried rice

PREP TIME 10 minutes · **COOK TIME** 20 minutes · **TOTAL TIME** 30 minutes · **SERVES** 4

My little sister and all my brothers adore this recipe. I can't tell you how often they ask me to make my fried rice. For a while, I didn't love most fried rice recipes. I felt like making it at home just never lived up to what you might order at a restaurant. But then, instead of following any kind of recipe, I just made my own version—one I knew I could love. My trick is using ground chicken, which cooks super quickly and mixes in wonderfully with the rice. Then I kick up the spice with fresh Thai chili peppers. I also add sushi-style pickled ginger and double up the amount of tamari. We like our rice really saucy. It's so delicious!

5 tablespoons untoasted sesame oil

½ pound ground chicken

3 green onions, thinly sliced, plus more for serving

2 to 3 Thai chilies, seeded, if desired, and chopped, plus more for serving

2 garlic cloves, chopped

2 cups roughly chopped Chinese broccoli or bok choy

½ cup loosely packed Thai or sweet basil leaves

⅓ cup pickled sushi ginger, drained

2 large eggs, beaten

Freshly ground black pepper

4 to 5 cups cooked jasmine rice

⅓ cup tamari or low-sodium soy sauce

2 tablespoons fish sauce

For Serving

Chopped peanuts

Thai basil

Lime wedges

1. In a large skillet, heat 2 tablespoons of the sesame oil over medium heat. When the oil is shimmering, add the chicken and cook, stirring, until it begins to brown, 4 to 5 minutes. Stir in the green onions, chilies, and garlic and cook until very fragrant, about 2 minutes more.

2. Add the broccoli, basil, and ginger. Cook, stirring occasionally, until the broccoli is bright green and the basil is wilted, 2 to 3 minutes. Move everything to one side of the pan, then add the eggs to the empty space. Gently scramble the eggs until they are softly set, 2 to 3 minutes. Season everything with pepper.

3. Add the remaining 3 tablespoons oil and the rice to the skillet. Cook without disturbing until the oil sizzles around the rice, about 5 minutes. Add the tamari and fish sauce. Toss well to combine, then remove from the heat.

4. Divide the rice among bowls and top with green onions, chilies, chopped peanuts, and Thai basil. Serve with lime wedges alongside.

creamy coconut chicken curry
with broccoli

PREP TIME 15 minutes, plus marinating time · COOK TIME See specific method · SERVES 6

Butter chicken is one of the most popular recipes that I've ever shared. I always use a good amount of spice in this dish, and I think that's why everyone loves it so much! But that recipe can take some time to make, so when I want something with similar flavors on busy weeknights, I make this curry. It's just as delicious. The trick is using a generous amount of garam masala to pack in the flavor. Then the garlic butter on top. It's not a traditional curry topping, but you can't go wrong with garlic butter. It makes everything yummier! As usual, I serve this curry with rice and soft naan. This dish is now a Gerard family favorite!

2 pounds boneless, skinless chicken thighs or breasts, cubed

1 medium yellow onion, diced

1 shallot, chopped

2 garlic cloves, chopped

1 (1-inch) piece fresh ginger, chopped or grated

2 tablespoons garam masala

2 teaspoons ground turmeric

1 teaspoon chili powder

Fine pink Himalayan salt

1 (6-ounce) can tomato paste

1 (14-ounce) can full-fat unsweetened coconut milk

4 cups chopped broccoli florets (from 1 medium head)

1/3 cup fresh cilantro, chopped

Cooked jasmine rice, for serving

Fresh naan, for serving

Garlic Butter

6 tablespoons (3/4 stick) salted butter

2 tablespoons sesame seeds

1 to 2 teaspoons crushed red pepper flakes

1/2 teaspoon smoked paprika

1 to 2 garlic cloves, chopped

SLOW COOKER
COOK TIME: 3 to 6 hours

1. In the bowl of your slow cooker, combine the chicken, onion, shallot, garlic, ginger, garam masala, turmeric, and chili powder. Season generously with salt. Toss to coat well and let marinate for about 10 minutes. Add the tomato paste and 1/3 cup water and stir to combine. Cover and cook on low for 5 to 6 hours or on high for 3 to 4 hours.

2. Increase the heat to high. Stir in the coconut milk and broccoli and cook, uncovered, until the broccoli is bright green and crisp-tender, about 12 minutes. Stir in the cilantro.

3. Meanwhile, make the garlic butter. In a small skillet over medium heat, melt together the butter, sesame seeds, red pepper flakes, and paprika. Cook, stirring, until the butter is just beginning to brown, 2 to 3 minutes. Add the garlic and cook until fragrant, 1 minute more. Remove from the heat.

4. Spoon the chicken and sauce over bowls of rice. Top with the garlic butter and serve with fresh naan.

STOVETOP
COOK TIME: 30 minutes

1. In a large Dutch oven, layer the onion and then the chicken. Add the shallot, garlic, ginger, garam masala, turmeric, and chili powder. Season generously with salt. Toss to coat and let marinate for about 10 minutes.

2. Add the tomato paste and 1/3 cup water. Place over medium heat and bring to a strong simmer. Partially cover and cook for about 10 minutes, then give everything a stir to incorporate, and continue cooking, partially covered, until the chicken is mostly opaque and almost cooked through, 10 minutes more.

3. Stir in the coconut milk, then add the broccoli. Reduce the heat to medium-low and cook uncovered, stirring occasionally, until the chicken is cooked through, the broccoli is bright green and crisp-tender, and the sauce is creamy, about 8 minutes more.

4. Make the garlic butter (see step 3, left). Spoon the chicken and sauce over bowls of rice, top with the garlic butter, and serve with fresh naan.

baked buffalo chicken tenders

PREP TIME 20 minutes · **COOK TIME** 20 minutes · **TOTAL TIME** 40 minutes · **SERVES** 4 to 6

Buffalo sauce is my specialty—and it is SO good on these baked chicken tenders. I have been making this sauce recipe for at least twelve years. You can't skip the butter—it's the key—and the seasonings add just the right amount of flavor. My brothers tell me it's the BEST buffalo sauce. Well, actually, according to them, it's "fire." They also love when I add a little chipotle chile powder, which adds smoke and more spice, if you're into that. Serve these saucy tenders with homemade ranch and a side of fries. I usually do sweet potato fries, which are my mom's favorite. Tenders + fries = everyone's favorite meal!

6 cups cornflakes

1/3 cup freshly grated
Parmesan cheese

1 teaspoon smoked paprika

1/2 teaspoon onion powder

1/2 teaspoon garlic powder

Fine pink Himalayan salt

2 large eggs

2 tablespoons hot sauce
(I like Frank's RedHot)

2 pounds boneless, skinless
chicken breast tenderloins

Extra-virgin olive oil

Homemade Buffalo Sauce
(recipe follows) or store-
bought buffalo sauce

Chopped fresh chives or green
onions, for serving (optional)

Homemade Ranch Dressing
(page 107) or store-bought
ranch dressing, for serving

1. Preheat the oven to 425°F. Line a baking sheet with parchment paper.

2. In a food processor, combine the cornflakes, Parmesan, paprika, onion powder, garlic powder, and a pinch of salt. Working in batches, if necessary, process into fine crumbs, 30 to 45 seconds. Alternatively, combine the ingredients in a large zip-top bag, seal it, and crush using your hands and/or a rolling pin. Transfer to a shallow bowl. Beat the eggs and hot sauce together in a large bowl.

3. Dip the chicken into the egg mixture and turn to coat, allowing excess to drip off. Dredge the chicken through the crumbs, covering to coat and pressing to adhere (see Note). Arrange on the prepared baking sheet. Lightly brush with olive oil.

4. Bake the chicken, flipping once halfway through, until cooked through and crisp all over, about 20 minutes.

5. Transfer the chicken to a serving platter. Drizzle the buffalo sauce over the top. Garnish with chives (if using) and serve with ranch dressing alongside for dipping.

homemade buffalo sauce

—————— **MAKES ABOUT 1 CUP** ——————

1/2 cup hot sauce (I like
Frank's RedHot)

8 tablespoons (1 stick)
salted butter, melted

1/2 teaspoon sweet paprika

1/2 teaspoon smoked paprika

1/2 teaspoon onion powder

1/2 teaspoon garlic powder

1/2 teaspoon fine pink
Himalayan salt

1/2 teaspoon freshly
ground black pepper

In a small bowl or lidded glass jar, combine the hot sauce, butter, sweet paprika, smoked paprika, onion powder, garlic powder, salt, and pepper. Whisk vigorously to combine. Store refrigerated for up to 2 weeks.

note: Double dredge the chicken for an even thicker coating: Double the amount of coating, dip the chicken back through the eggs, then through the crumbs a second time.

garlic mushroom chicken skillet

PREP TIME 10 minutes · **COOK TIME** 30 minutes · **TOTAL TIME** 40 minutes · **SERVES** 6

Let me tell you—this skillet almost didn't make it into the book. I added it in the eleventh hour (literally), because it was just too delicious to leave out! This is THE most flavorful chicken. It's so good and has just the right amount of garlic. The mushrooms are perfectly cooked with some balsamic vinegar. And the white wine sauce? It is to die for—you must serve this with bread for soaking up every bit of that sauce! And I love to finish this dish with crispy prosciutto on top. It seals the deal!

3 tablespoons extra-virgin olive oil

4 ounces thinly sliced prosciutto

1½ pounds boneless, skinless chicken thighs or breasts

1 tablespoon chopped fresh sage

1 teaspoon onion powder

1 teaspoon garlic powder

Fine pink Himalayan salt and freshly ground black pepper

6 tablespoons (¾ stick) salted butter

12 ounces shiitake and/or cremini mushrooms, sliced

4 garlic cloves, chopped

2 tablespoons fresh thyme leaves, plus more for serving

Crushed red pepper flakes

3 tablespoons balsamic vinegar

1 cup low-sodium chicken broth

¾ cup dry white wine, such as pinot grigio or sauvignon blanc

Crusty bread, for serving (optional)

1. Place a large skillet over medium-high heat and add 2 tablespoons of the olive oil. When the oil is shimmering, add the prosciutto and cook, stirring occasionally, until crisped, about 5 minutes. Transfer the prosciutto to a plate.

2. To the same skillet over medium-high heat, add the remaining tablespoon olive oil, then the chicken, sage, onion powder, and garlic powder and season with salt and pepper. Toss to coat, then sear the chicken, without turning, until it is golden on the bottom, 3 to 5 minutes. Flip the chicken and cook for 2 more minutes to brown. Add 2 tablespoons of the butter, letting it melt and lightly brown around the chicken, 2 to 3 minutes. Transfer the chicken to the plate with the prosciutto, reserving the butter and oil in the pan.

3. Place the same skillet over medium-low heat and add the mushrooms. Cook undisturbed until golden, about 5 to 8 minutes. Add the remaining 4 tablespoons butter, the garlic, thyme, and a pinch each of salt, black pepper, and red pepper flakes. Cook, stirring, until softened and fragrant, 3 to 4 minutes. Pour in the vinegar and cook, stirring and scraping up any browned bits from the bottom of the pan, about 1 minute.

4. Pour in the broth and wine, then return the chicken to the pan. Cook, turning occasionally, until the chicken is warmed through and the sauce slightly thickened, 6 to 8 minutes.

5. Serve family style, topped with the crispy prosciutto and thyme and crusty bread alongside for dipping, if desired.

sesame-crusted chicken schnitzel "pizza"

PREP TIME 15 minutes · **COOK TIME** 15 minutes · **TOTAL TIME** 30 minutes · **SERVES** 6

I cannot tell you where the idea for this recipe came from, but as soon as it entered my mind, I knew it would be a standout. Picture this: a thin and crispy piece of chicken schnitzel topped with the best homemade pizza seasoning, plus marinara, cheese, and pepperoni. I immediately created the dish that night, and, as expected, everyone loved it—especially Creighton, who says it's both super delicious and super unique. Be sure to pound out your chicken cutlets as thin as you can—you want a nice base for the sauce and cheese to land on.

¾ cup all-purpose flour

3 large eggs

2 cups panko breadcrumbs

1 cup sesame seeds

1 tablespoon Homemade Seasoned Salt (page 56) or store-bought seasoned salt

Freshly ground black pepper

6 chicken cutlets, or 3 boneless, skinless chicken breasts, halved horizontally

Avocado oil, for frying

2 tablespoons Homemade Pizza Seasoning (recipe follows) or store-bought pizza seasoning, plus more for serving

1 cup marinara sauce (I like Rao's)

1½ cups shredded provolone cheese

2 ounces thinly sliced pepperoni

Fresh basil leaves, for serving

1. Preheat the oven to 400°F. Line a baking sheet with parchment paper.

2. Place the flour in a shallow dish. Beat the eggs in a separate shallow dish. In a third shallow dish, combine the panko, sesame seeds, seasoned salt, and pepper. Line up the dishes in this order.

3. Dredge each piece of the chicken in the flour, turning to coat both sides. Dip the chicken into the eggs and turn to coat, allowing excess to drip off. Dredge the chicken through the panko mixture, covering to coat and pressing to adhere. Transfer the coated pieces to a plate.

4. In a large skillet over medium-high heat, add about half an inch of oil. When the oil is shimmering, add the chicken, in batches as necessary, and cook until golden brown on the bottom, about 3 minutes. Flip the chicken and cook until golden brown all over, 3 minutes more. Transfer the chicken to the prepared baking sheet.

5. Sprinkle the chicken with the pizza seasoning, then spoon the marinara sauce over the top, dividing it evenly. Top with the cheese, then the pepperoni. Bake until the cheese is melted and bubbling lightly, 7 to 10 minutes.

6. Finish the schnitzel with basil and more pizza seasoning before serving.

homemade pizza seasoning

———— **MAKES ABOUT ½ CUP** ————

½ cup freshly grated Parmesan cheese

2 tablespoons sesame seeds

2 tablespoons Homemade Italian Seasoning (page 128) or store-bought Italian seasoning

Crushed red pepper flakes

In a glass jar, combine the Parmesan, sesame seeds, Italian seasoning, and red pepper flakes. Stir to combine well. Seal and store refrigerated for up to 2 weeks.

herby sun-dried tomato chicken

PREP TIME 10 minutes · **COOK TIME** 20 minutes · **TOTAL TIME** 30 minutes · **SERVES** 4

This is that perfect any-night-of-the-week skillet dinner. It is saucy and cheesy, and I think it's best served with some kind of bread for mopping up the delicious pan sauce. Then lots of fresh basil scattered all over the dish. And while the wine creates a wonderful sauce, if you prefer to not cook with alcohol, try replacing it with apple cider or white grape juice. Both are a little sweeter, which is great! Oh, and one last tip: If you make this in the summer, replace the sun-dried tomatoes in the pesto with juicy fresh peaches—yes, peaches! They are so yummy in the wine sauce.

1 to 1½ pounds boneless, skinless chicken thighs or breasts

3 tablespoons extra-virgin olive oil

½ cup Sun-Dried Tomato Pesto (recipe follows) or store-bought sun-dried tomato pesto

2 tablespoons fresh thyme leaves

2 teaspoons chopped fresh rosemary

Fine pink Himalayan salt and freshly ground black pepper

2 garlic cloves, chopped

1½ cups dry white wine, such as pinot grigio or sauvignon blanc

5 ounces fresh baby spinach

8 ounces low-moisture whole-milk mozzarella cheese, torn

½ cup loosely packed fresh basil leaves, torn

1. Preheat the oven to 425°F.

2. Rub the chicken all over with 2 tablespoons of the olive oil, the sun-dried tomato pesto, thyme, and rosemary and season generously with salt and pepper. Place a cast-iron skillet over medium-high heat. When it is hot, add the chicken. Cook until both sides are golden brown, 3 to 4 minutes per side.

3. Reduce the heat to medium-low, then add the remaining 1 tablespoon olive oil and the garlic. Pour in the wine, then add the spinach. Simmer until the chicken is cooked through, about 5 minutes. Arrange the mozzarella around the chicken.

4. Transfer to the oven and bake for 5 minutes, then turn on the broiler and continue cooking until bubbly, about 5 minutes more.

5. Serve the chicken with the pan sauce and basil.

sun-dried tomato pesto

— MAKES 1 CUP —

1 cup fresh basil

½ cup oil-packed sun-dried tomatoes, plus ½ cup oil from the jar

2 tablespoons toasted pine nuts, walnuts, or seed of your choice

½ cup freshly grated Parmesan cheese

Zest and juice of 1 lemon

Fine pink Himalayan salt

Crushed red pepper flakes

In a blender or food processor, combine the basil, sun-dried tomatoes and oil, pine nuts, Parmesan, and lemon zest and juice. Season with salt and red pepper flakes. Pulse until smooth but still a little chunky, about 10 pulses. Taste and adjust the seasonings as needed. Store in an airtight container in the refrigerator for up to 2 weeks.

baked cajun chicken skewers
with garlic parmesan sauce

PREP TIME 10 minutes · COOK TIME 20 minutes · TOTAL TIME 30 minutes · SERVES 4 to 6

My family has a cabin in Ripley, New York, and we would often spend our weekends there growing up. On the two-hour drive back home to Cleveland, my brothers could sometimes convince my parents to stop at the Quaker Steak & Lube, a car-themed burgers and chicken wing restaurant. They loved their wings, fries, and ALL the hot sauces. My mom and I would always order boneless wings with the Cajun seasoning and sauce. I took the memory of those flavors and created these chicken skewers, which my mom says are even better! We love this garlic Parmesan sauce for dipping and dunking, plus you've got to have a side of homemade baked sweet potato fries. So delicious and great—but a little bit unexpected—for game day!

2 tablespoons extra-virgin olive oil, plus more for greasing

2 pounds boneless, skinless chicken thighs or breasts, cut into 1-inch cubes

2 tablespoons freshly grated Parmesan cheese

2 tablespoons Homemade Cajun Seasoning (page 235) or store-bought Cajun seasoning

1 teaspoon smoked paprika

1 teaspoon onion powder

1 teaspoon garlic powder

Fine pink Himalayan salt and freshly ground black pepper

Chopped fresh cilantro, for serving

Garlic Parmesan Sauce

$\frac{1}{2}$ cup mayonnaise

1 to 2 garlic cloves, finely chopped or grated

$\frac{1}{2}$ cup freshly grated Parmesan cheese

1 teaspoon fresh lemon juice

1. Preheat the oven to 450°F.

2. On the prepared baking sheet, toss together the chicken, olive oil, Parmesan, Cajun seasoning, paprika, onion powder, and garlic powder, and season with salt and pepper. Thread the chicken onto 4 to 6 metal skewers, leaving a little space between each piece. Arrange the skewers on the baking sheet, spacing them at least 1 inch apart.

3. Bake until the chicken is opaque and cooked through, 15 to 20 minutes.

4. **Meanwhile, make the garlic Parmesan sauce.** In a medium bowl, combine the mayo, garlic, Parmesan, and lemon juice. Stir to mix well. Season with salt and pepper as needed.

5. Transfer the chicken skewers to a platter and sprinkle with cilantro. Serve with the sauce alongside.

sheet pan oregano chicken
with herby citrus sauce

PREP TIME 30 minutes · **COOK TIME** 30 minutes · **TOTAL TIME** 1 hour · **SERVES** 4 to 6

Sheet pan dinners are just the best. They are easy to make and, to me, the outcome is always delicious. Why? Cooking everything together on one pan allows the flavors from each element of the dish to meld to create maximum tastiness! And that's surely the case with this oregano chicken. The Cuban-inspired seasoning on the chicken has lots of fresh oregano, cumin, and a mix of both orange and lime zests. The herby sauce also has lots of citrus, which is essential to Cuban cooking and, of course, so delicious! Serve this chicken topped with avocado salsa for a layer of creaminess. All together, every bite is such a good flavor bomb. And while this dish is great all year long, I especially love it in the winter and early spring, when citrus is at its peak.

Chicken

1½ pounds boneless, skinless chicken thighs or breasts

4 tablespoons extra-virgin olive oil

6 garlic cloves, finely chopped or grated

2 tablespoons chopped fresh oregano

1 tablespoon orange zest

1 tablespoon lime zest

1 teaspoon ground cumin

½ teaspoon cayenne pepper

Fine pink Himalayan salt and freshly ground black pepper

1 medium yellow onion, sliced

2 russet potatoes, cut into wedges

1 poblano pepper, sliced

Herby Citrus Sauce

⅓ cup extra-virgin olive oil

⅓ cup fresh orange juice

¼ cup fresh lime juice

¼ cup fresh cilantro

Crushed red pepper flakes

Fine pink Himalayan salt

Smashed Avocado Salsa

1 avocado, diced

½ cup fresh cilantro, chopped

1 jalapeño, seeded and chopped

2 green onions, thinly sliced

2 tablespoons fresh lime juice

Fine pink Himalayan salt

1. Make the chicken. Preheat the oven to 425°F.

2. On a baking sheet, combine the chicken, 2 tablespoons of the olive oil, the garlic, oregano, orange zest, lime zest, cumin, and cayenne. Season with salt and pepper and toss to coat well. Add the onion, potatoes, and poblano around the chicken and toss with the remaining 2 tablespoons olive oil and additional salt and pepper.

3. Spread the chicken and vegetables in an even layer. Bake until the chicken is cooked and the potatoes golden, about 30 minutes, tossing halfway through.

4. Meanwhile, make the sauce. In a blender or food processor, combine the olive oil, orange juice, lime juice, cilantro, and red pepper flakes. Season with salt and blend on high speed until well combined and pale in color, about 1 minute. Taste and adjust the seasonings as needed.

5. Make the salsa. In a medium bowl, combine the avocado, cilantro, jalapeño, green onions, and lime juice. Season with salt. Gently smash with a fork, leaving the texture a bit chunky.

6. Arrange the chicken on a serving platter. Spoon the citrus sauce all over, then add a dollop of the salsa on top of each serving.

sage butter–fried pork chops
with sherry pan sauce

PREP TIME 10 minutes · **COOK TIME** 20 minutes · **TOTAL TIME** 30 minutes · **SERVES** 4

I don't make pork chops very often, but when I do, this is my go-to. It's the sherry sauce that makes these chops SO GOOD. It's salty and tangy with the slightest bit of sweetness from fig preserves. I think figs and pork make the yummiest combo, and they're not paired up enough in my opinion! In the fall, try adding thinly sliced apples (in step 2, with the shallots). Such a cozy dinner. And don't forget to serve these pork chops with crusty bread—it's delish dipped in the sherry sauce.

4 (1-inch-thick) bone-in pork chops

Fine pink Himalayan salt and freshly ground black pepper

4 tablespoons (½ stick) salted butter

2 shallots, quartered

12 fresh sage leaves

4 fresh thyme sprigs

1 cup dry white wine, such as pinot grigio or sauvignon blanc

½ cup dry sherry

2 tablespoons fig preserves

½ teaspoon cayenne pepper

Crushed red pepper flakes

1. Season the pork chops all over with salt and pepper. Melt 1 tablespoon of the butter in a large skillet over medium-high heat. Add the pork chops and cook, turning once, until nicely browned, 2 to 3 minutes per side.

2. Add the remaining 3 tablespoons butter, the shallots, sage, and thyme to the pan, tilting the pan to swirl the butter around the chops. Continue cooking, spooning the butter over the chops, until the pork is cooked through and the shallots have softened, 4 to 5 minutes. Transfer the pork and fried herbs to a plate, reserving the shallots in the pan.

3. To the same skillet over medium-high heat, add the wine and sherry, and cook, using a wooden spoon to scrape up any browned bits from the bottom of the pan, until reduced by about half, 2 to 3 minutes. Add the fig preserves and cayenne and season with salt, black pepper, and red pepper flakes. Cook, stirring occasionally, until the sauce has thickened slightly, about 5 minutes.

4. Return the pork chops to the pan along with any collected juices and cook, spooning the sauce over the top, just long enough to warm through, 2 to 3 minutes. Serve the chops with the sauce and fried herbs.

beef

garlic butter steak bites
with bang bang sauce

PREP TIME 15 minutes · **COOK TIME** 15 minutes · **TOTAL TIME** 30 minutes · **SERVES** 6

Well, these steak bites are just delicious—and so fast to make! Be sure to use a flavorful cut of meat. My family is super into a great rib-eye, but whatever you love will work. The idea is to make your skillet super hot so you get a great sear on the meat, then add butter, tamari, and garlic to coat each delicious bite. The garlicky butter sauce is what makes this REALLY irresistible. And the bang bang sauce to go with it is a must-make. Sweet chili sauce mixed with mayo is a winning combo every time. No one will complain when you serve these bites—the dish is always a hit. Stick toothpicks in the bites and serve them as an appetizer, or add a side of rice for dinner.

1 tablespoon extra-virgin olive oil

2 pounds beef tenderloin or rib-eye steak, cut into large cubes

Freshly ground black pepper

6 tablespoons (¾ stick) cold salted butter, cubed

¼ cup tamari or low-sodium soy sauce

4 garlic cloves, chopped

¼ cup pickled sushi ginger, drained

Chopped Thai basil or cilantro, for serving

Bang Bang Sauce

½ cup mayonnaise

⅓ cup sweet Thai chili sauce

2 tablespoons tamari or low-sodium soy sauce

1 garlic clove, finely chopped or grated

2 teaspoons lime zest plus 1 tablespoon fresh lime juice

1 tablespoon chopped pickled sushi ginger

1. Place a large skillet over high heat and add the olive oil. Pat the steak dry and season all over with pepper. Add the steak to the pan and cook, undisturbed, until it is well-browned on the bottom, 3 to 5 minutes. Stir and cook, until the steak is browned on all sides, 3 to 5 minutes more. Add the butter, tamari, garlic, and ginger and toss to coat. Cook until the garlic is fragrant, 2 to 3 minutes more.

2. Meanwhile, make the bang bang sauce. In a medium bowl, combine the mayo, chili sauce, tamari, garlic, lime zest, lime juice, and pickled ginger. Stir to combine well.

3. Sprinkle the Thai basil over the beef and spoon the garlic butter over the top. Serve with the bang bang sauce alongside for dipping.

cider-braised beef brisket

PREP TIME 15 minutes · **COOK TIME** 3 hours 35 minutes · **TOTAL TIME** 3 hours 50 minutes · **SERVES** 6 to 8

For the longest time, I steered clear of cooking any kind of brisket. I wasn't familiar with cooking it and, honestly, I know this is silly, but the thought of photographing a brisket made me a little nervous! How could I make a brisket look SO YUMMY, you know? But I finally put all that aside and listened to Creighton, who has made many requests for it. I made it just for him, but I was so pleasantly surprised with the deliciousness and ease of the recipe that I had to share it with you. And now it has become a staple dish! Serve it with potatoes or over rice, or use the meat in sandwiches. This brisket is so versatile!

1 (5-pound) beef brisket

Fine pink Himalayan salt and freshly ground black pepper

2 tablespoons all-purpose flour

2 tablespoons salted butter

3 medium yellow onions, thinly sliced

4 shallots, halved

2 cups apple cider, plus more as needed

2 tablespoons fresh thyme leaves

3 cups dry white wine, such as pinot grigio or sauvignon blanc, or low-sodium beef broth

1½ pounds baby carrots

8 garlic cloves, smashed

2 tablespoons Maple Apple Butter (recipe follows) or store-bought apple butter

Flaky sea salt, for serving

1. Preheat the oven to 375°F.

2. Season the brisket all over with salt and pepper, then rub with the flour to coat. Heat a large Dutch oven over high heat. Add the butter and the onions and cook, stirring, until they are soft and beginning to color, about 5 minutes. Add the shallots and ½ cup of the apple cider. Season with salt and pepper. Continue cooking, stirring occasionally, until the onions are evenly browned and most of the cider has evaporated, 5 to 8 minutes more. Add the thyme and cook until fragrant, about 1 minute.

3. Snuggle the brisket, fat-side down, in among the onions. Add the remaining 1½ cups of cider and the wine and bring to a simmer over medium-high heat, adding more cider if needed to keep the meat mostly covered. Arrange the carrots and garlic around the brisket. Cover and carefully transfer to the oven. Bake until the meat is tender throughout, about 3 hours.

4. Increase the oven temperature to 425°F. Uncover the brisket and coat the top with the apple butter. Continue to bake, uncovered, until the top is deeply caramelized, 20 to 30 minutes more, adding cider as needed to keep the onions moist but just barely covered with liquid.

5. Remove the brisket from the pot, place on a cutting board, and tent with aluminum foil. Let stand 10 minutes. With a sharp knife, slice the meat against the grain. Transfer to a platter. Sprinkle the meat with flaky salt and serve the onions, carrots, and pan juices on the side.

maple apple butter

4 pounds Honeycrisp apples, cored and diced

1¼ cups apple cider

½ cup maple syrup, plus more as needed

1 tablespoon pure vanilla extract

2 cinnamon sticks, or 2 teaspoons ground cinnamon

1 teaspoon ground ginger

½ teaspoon freshly grated nutmeg

¼ teaspoon ground cloves

Fine pink Himalayan salt

In a large heavy-bottomed pot over high heat, combine the apples, apple cider, maple syrup, vanilla, cinnamon sticks, ginger, nutmeg, cloves, salt, and 1 cup of water. Bring to a boil, then reduce the heat to medium-low. Cook, stirring occasionally, until the apples are softened completely and the liquid has reduced by half, 30 to 40 minutes, adding more water as needed to keep the apples submerged. Remove the pot from the heat and let cool slightly. Discard the cinnamon sticks, then transfer the apples to a blender or food processer and puree until smooth. Return the mixture to the pot and cook over medium heat until slightly thickened, 15 to 20 minutes. Taste and add more maple syrup as needed. Let cool, then transfer the apple butter to an airtight container and store in the refrigerator for up to 1 month.

double-baked taquitos

PREP TIME 25 minutes · **COOK TIME** 40 minutes · **TOTAL TIME** 1 hour 5 minutes · **SERVES** 6

It's no secret my family loves a crispy taco—I grew up eating my dad's crispy tacos once or sometimes even twice a week. They're still the whole family's favorite meal today! Needless to say, we also love taquitos—but these taquitos are special. I always bake them, as opposed to frying them, because it's so much easier. And then, just like Dad does with his tacos, I bake them a second time. The first bake gets them crispy, then we add cheese and bake again until it's melty and crispy around the edges. The toppings totally make it . . . a dollop of yogurt or sour cream, lots of avocado, and a generous sprinkle of fresh cilantro, plus a big squeeze of lime juice. YUM!

1 pound lean ground beef

1 yellow onion, chopped

3 tablespoons Homemade Taco Seasoning (recipe follows) or store-bought taco seasoning

2 cups red enchilada sauce

4 ounces cream cheese, at room temperature, cut into pieces

16 to 20 corn tortillas

Extra-virgin olive oil, for coating

2 cups shredded Mexican cheese blend

2 avocados, chopped

⅓ cup chopped fresh cilantro

1 jalapeño, seeded, if desired, and chopped

¼ cup fresh lime juice, plus lime wedges for serving

Flaky sea salt

Sour cream or plain Greek yogurt, for serving

1. Preheat the oven to 425°F.

2. In a large skillet set over medium-high heat, place the beef and onion. Cook, breaking up the meat with a wooden spoon, until the fat has rendered and the beef is browned, 8 to 10 minutes. Add the taco seasoning and ¾ cup water. Reduce the heat to medium and simmer until the sauce thickens to coat the meat, about 5 minutes. Stir in ½ cup of the enchilada sauce and the cream cheese. Cook, stirring, just until the cream cheese melts, 1 to 2 minutes. Remove the skillet from the heat.

3. Working in batches, warm the tortillas in the microwave in 30-second intervals until pliable. Place the tortillas on a baking sheet and rub one side with olive oil. Flip them over and spoon 2 tablespoons of the beef mixture down the center of each on the unoiled side. Roll up the tortilla as for a cigar and place seam-side down on the baking sheet. Repeat with the remaining tortillas and beef.

4. Bake the taquitos until they begin to crisp, about 10 minutes, then carefully flip them over and cook until crispy, 4 to 5 minutes. Remove from the oven, leaving the temperature set at 425°F.

5. Coat the bottom of a 9 x 13-inch baking dish with 1 cup of the enchilada sauce. Arrange the taquitos over the sauce and top with the remaining ½ cup enchilada sauce and then the shredded cheese. Bake until the cheese is melted and bubbling, 8 to 10 minutes.

6. Meanwhile, in a medium bowl, combine the avocados, cilantro, jalapeño, lime juice, and a pinch of flaky salt. Stir gently to mix.

7. Top the taquitos with the avocado mixture and sour cream. Serve warm with lime wedges for squeezing.

homemade taco seasoning

———— **MAKES ABOUT ½ CUP** ————

2 tablespoons chili powder

1 tablespoon chipotle chile powder

1 tablespoon smoked paprika

1 tablespoon garlic powder

1 tablespoon onion powder

2 teaspoons ground cumin

1 teaspoon dried oregano

1 teaspoon fine pink Himalayan salt

In a glass jar, combine the chili powder, chipotle chile powder, paprika, garlic powder, onion powder, cumin, oregano, and salt. Stir to mix well. Store at room temperature in a cool, dark place for up to 6 months.

nonnie's chili

PREP TIME 20 minutes · **COOK TIME** 2 hours · **TOTAL TIME** 2 hours 20 minutes · **SERVES** 6

I talk about my Nonnie a lot. She has inspired so much of what I do today, and that includes many of my recipes. This is my version of her chili, and it's now the only chili recipe I make—it's my family's favorite. Nonnie kept things simple and so easy. She was a NO-FUSS kind of cook and baker. Her chili is made with a simple seasoning blend that she swore by. The secret is using both chili powder and chipotle chile powder for the most flavor. And then the key is homemade beer bread for serving! Nonnie started her chili an hour before dinnertime because that was just her style, but I like to cook mine all day and let it simmer so the aroma fills the house. It's so cozy!

2 pounds lean ground beef, bison, and/or chicken

2 small yellow onions, chopped

2 bell peppers, any color, chopped

2 tablespoons chili powder

1 tablespoon chipotle chile powder

1 tablespoon smoked paprika

1 tablespoon dried oregano

1 tablespoon garlic powder

2 teaspoons ground cumin

Fine pink Himalayan salt and freshly ground black pepper

4 cups low-sodium beef broth, plus more as needed

1 (28-ounce) can crushed tomatoes

1 (6-ounce) can tomato paste

2 (4-ounce) cans diced green chiles

½ cup pickled jalapeños, chopped

1 tablespoon Worcestershire sauce

1 (14-ounce) can pinto or black beans

For Serving

Plain Greek yogurt

Shredded cheddar cheese

Sliced avocado

Thinly sliced green onion

Chopped fresh cilantro

Oyster crackers

1. Place the beef and onions in a large Dutch oven. Cook over medium-high heat, breaking up the beef with a wooden spoon, until the beef is browned and the onions are beginning to soften, about 10 minutes. Add the bell peppers, chili powder, chipotle chile powder, paprika, oregano, garlic powder, cumin, and 1½ teaspoons salt. Stir to coat.

2. Add 4 cups of broth, the tomatoes, tomato paste, green chiles, jalapeños, and Worcestershire. Season with salt and pepper. Increase the heat to high and bring to a boil, then reduce the heat to low. Partially cover and cook, stirring occasionally, until the flavors are melded and the chili has reached your desired thickness, 2 to 3 hours. Add more broth as needed if the mixture becomes dry.

3. Just before serving, stir in the beans and cook to heat them through, 1 to 2 minutes. Spoon the chili into bowls and top as desired.

smash burgers
with special sauce

PREP TIME 30 minutes · COOK TIME 15 minutes · TOTAL TIME 45 minutes, plus chilling time · MAKES 8 burgers

This burger! My love for the burger is strong—and Creighton LOVES a great burger, too, but he especially loves this one. A while back, he asked me to make smash burgers. They sounded fun, so I started making them, and over time I perfected our ideal version. I season the meat with a little bit of fish sauce, which adds a delicious saltiness. But also—the special sauce. It's so good, you have to double it. The chopped-up pickles are so yummy! I layer my smash burger TALL. Toasted brioche buns (ideally with sesame seeds) get a thin layer of special sauce. I add one or two patties (my brothers always want double patties), then shredded lettuce, pickles, and extra special sauce on top. Be sure you use sharp or spicy cheddar slices here. Classic smash burgers use American cheese, but these work best with REAL, delicious cheddar. Trust me. Then, of course, you have to do fries on the side to complete the smash burger experience!

2 pounds lean ground beef

8 tablespoons (1 stick) salted butter, melted, plus more at room temperature for buns

2 tablespoons Worcestershire sauce

2 teaspoons fish sauce

2 teaspoons smoked paprika

1 teaspoon onion powder

1 teaspoon garlic powder

Freshly ground black pepper

8 sesame brioche buns

8 slices cheddar cheese

Special Sauce

1/2 cup mayonnaise

2 tablespoons ketchup

2 tablespoons finely chopped dill pickles

1 to 2 tablespoons hot sauce (I like Frank's RedHot)

2 teaspoons prepared horseradish

1 teaspoon Worcestershire sauce

1 garlic clove, finely chopped or grated

Fine pink Himalayan salt and freshly ground black pepper

Toppings

Shredded romaine lettuce

Sliced tomatoes

Sliced dill pickles

Red onion slices or Pickled Red Onions (see page 156)

1. In a large bowl, combine the beef, melted butter, Worcestershire, fish sauce, paprika, onion powder, garlic powder, and a generous pinch of pepper. Use your hands to mix well, then form into 8 even balls. Place on a plate or baking sheet and refrigerate for at least 15 minutes or overnight.

2. **Meanwhile, make the special sauce.** In a medium bowl, combine the mayo, ketchup, pickles, hot sauce, horseradish, Worcestershire, and garlic. Season with salt and pepper and stir to mix well.

3. Heat a cast-iron skillet, griddle, or outdoor grill to high heat. Cut 8 squares of parchment paper that are a little larger than your burger buns.

4. Butter the insides of the buns. Working in batches, place in the skillet buttered sides down and toast until just crispy and warmed through, 2 to 3 minutes. Slather the toasted buns with the special sauce.

5. Return the skillet to high heat. Working in batches, add the chilled burger balls to the hot skillet. Cook for about 20 seconds, then place a parchment square on top of each burger. Using a flat metal spatula or cast-iron press, smash down on the burgers hard and fast to get them as flat as you can in one motion—they'll be sizzling. Cook until the bottoms begin to brown, about 1 minute, then flip, top with cheese, and cook until the cheese is melting and the burgers are just cooked through, about 2 minutes more.

6. Slide the smash burgers onto the bottom buns and top as desired. Finish with the top buns and serve immediately.

pan-seared buttery rib-eyes

PREP TIME 5 minutes · COOK TIME 10 minutes · TOTAL TIME 15 minutes, plus resting time · SERVES 2

Ask any of my brothers, and they will most likely tell you this is their favorite recipe of mine. They literally crave these rib-eyes, and I can't deny it: they are definitely crave-worthy. The buttery, herby sauce around each steak has the richest, most delicious flavor. You can't beat it. If possible, use organic, grass-fed, cultured butter that is cold from the fridge. Cultured butter is fermented cream, then churned to 82% butter fat, which gives the butter an incredible taste, making it ideal for browning. I love the Straus Family Creamery brand. Serve these rib-eyes with a big salad, like the Mean Green Salad (page 82) or the Sage Chicken & Apple Salad with Harvest Vinaigrette—just leave the chicken out (page 78). To make it a perfect meal, do Mom's Cheesy Potato Casserole (page 137) or a side of Sheet Pan Mac & Cheese (page 124). Wow, YUM!

2 (1¼-pound) bone-in rib-eye steaks (about 1½ inches thick)

Fine pink Himalayan salt and freshly ground black pepper

6 tablespoons (¾ stick) cold salted butter, cubed

6 garlic cloves, smashed

1 shallot, peeled and quartered

4 thyme sprigs

1 rosemary sprig

Flaky sea salt, for serving

1. Pat the steaks dry and season both sides with salt and pepper. Let them rest at room temperature for 30 to 40 minutes.

2. Heat a large cast-iron skillet over high heat. When it is just smoking, place the steaks in the skillet and cook until deeply browned on the bottom, 4 to 5 minutes. Flip them and add the butter, garlic, shallot, thyme, and rosemary, scattering them around the pan. Cook, spooning the melted butter over the steaks, until the outside is browned all over and the inside is medium-rare, about 5 minutes more, or longer if you prefer your steak more well-done (see Note).

3. Transfer the steaks to a cutting board and let rest for 5 minutes before slicing. Serve with the brown butter and fried herbs spooned over the top. Finish with flaky salt.

note: You can use a meat thermometer to check for the doneness of your steak and ensure it's cooked to your version of perfection. I like mine medium-rare, but you can cook yours as short or long as you like!

Medium-rare: 135°F   Medium: 145°F

Medium-well: 150°F   Well done: 160°F

cheeseburger pasta

PREP TIME 10 minutes · **COOK TIME** 20 minutes · **TOTAL TIME** 30 minutes · **SERVES** 6

I only make this pasta when Creighton is around—it is one of his ALL-time favorites. Actually, it's very similar to the first dish I ever cooked for him, which was a chili mac and cheese. Of course, he also loves a really good cheeseburger, and he constantly requests that I create a homemade version of Hamburger Helper. So I finally did! My version of the old-school family favorite dinner is a tad spicier: I use a mix of chili powder, smoked paprika, and jalapeños to give this creamy pasta a nice kick. Creighton loves the additional heat, since nothing is ever too spicy for him! This dish is made in one pot and can be ready in around 30 minutes. It's great for busy weeknights when you still want a ton of flavor!

1 pound lean ground beef

1 medium yellow
onion, chopped

Fine pink Himalayan salt and
freshly ground black pepper

2 teaspoons smoked
or sweet paprika

1 teaspoon chili powder

1 teaspoon garlic powder

2 cups low-sodium beef
or chicken broth

⅓ cup ketchup

¼ cup chopped dill pickles

¼ cup chopped
pickled jalapeños

2 tablespoons yellow mustard

1 pound short-cut pasta,
such as elbow macaroni

1 cup milk of your choice

1½ to 2 cups shredded
cheddar cheese

Finely chopped fresh parsley
and/or basil, for serving

1. Place the beef and onion in a Dutch oven set over medium heat. Season with salt and pepper. Cook, breaking up the meat with a wooden spoon, until the meat is browned and cooked through and the onion is soft, 8 to 10 minutes. Stir in the paprika, chili powder, and garlic powder and cook until fragrant, 1 minute more.

2. Pour in the broth and 1½ cups water. Stir in the ketchup, pickles, jalapeños, and mustard. Add the pasta and season with salt. Increase the heat to high and bring to a boil, then reduce the heat to medium-low and cook, stirring often, until the pasta is al dente, 5 to 8 minutes. Stir in the milk, then the cheese and cook until everything is melty and warmed through, 2 to 3 minutes more.

3. Divide the pasta among bowls and top with fresh herbs before serving.

red chile beef tostadas
with cotija eggs

PREP TIME 10 minutes · COOK TIME 20 minutes · TOTAL TIME 30 minutes · SERVES 4

My family loves a great Mexican-inspired dinner—we usually have tacos or enchiladas once or even twice a week. No one in my family will ever complain about a taco night, but when I feel like changing things up, I love to make tostadas. These are so delicious! Picture a crisp tortilla piled with beef and topped with an egg poached directly in the red chile sauce. It's so much easier than frying half a dozen eggs, plus the eggs come out silkier this way. They're perfect for topping each crispy cheesy tostada. ALL of my brothers have given these double thumbs up. We just love them for that!

6 to 8 tostada shells

1 pound lean ground beef

1 yellow onion, chopped

2 teaspoons chili powder

2 teaspoons smoked paprika

1 teaspoon ground cumin

Fine pink Himalayan salt and freshly ground black pepper

2 cups red enchilada sauce

1 to 2 cups shredded Mexican cheese blend

6 to 8 large eggs

1/3 cup crumbled cotija cheese

2 avocados, diced

1 cup fresh cilantro, chopped

2 green onions, thinly sliced

2 tablespoons fresh lime juice

1 jalapeño, seeded, if desired, and chopped

1. Preheat the oven to 400°F. Arrange the tostada shells on a baking sheet.

2. In a large skillet set over high heat, combine the ground beef and the onion and cook, breaking up the meat with a wooden spoon, until it is browned and the onion is soft and translucent, about 8 minutes. Add the chili powder, paprika, and cumin and season with salt and pepper. Cook until fragrant, 1 to 2 minutes more. Remove the skillet from the heat. Stir in 1 cup of the enchilada sauce.

3. Spoon the meat over the tostada shells, dividing evenly. Top with the Mexican cheese blend. Bake until the cheese is melted, 5 to 7 minutes.

4. Meanwhile, cook the eggs. Return the skillet from the beef to medium heat (no need to wipe it out). Working quickly, in batches as necessary, add the remaining 1 cup enchilada sauce in 6 to 8 small mounds. (It will sizzle; be careful.) Crack the eggs directly into the center of each. Cook until the whites are set, 4 to 5 minutes, sprinkling the cotija cheese around the edges of the eggs during the last minute or so to melt the cheese.

5. In a medium bowl, combine the avocados, cilantro, green onions, lime juice and jalapeño. Season with salt and stir to mix.

6. Slide the eggs and cheese onto each tostada. Top with the avocado mixture and serve immediately.

saucy, spicy, cheesy oven-baked meatballs

PREP TIME 25 minutes · **COOK TIME** 30 minutes · **TOTAL TIME** 55 minutes · **SERVES** 6 to 8

I know I say this about a lot of things, but these meatballs are truly *delicious*. They are one of the recipes that inspired the idea of creating this entire book! They're very quick and very cozy. I have kept these shortcut meatballs a secret for years, but I make them all the time in the fall and winter. The trick here is a mix of ground beef and spicy Italian sausage. The sausage adds flavor without having to add more ingredients. Then, the surprise: chili paste. Of course, it's not traditional in an Italian-style meatball, but the hit of spice and tang is what makes these next level, even if you might not know exactly what it's coming from. Serve these meatballs with creamy polenta or a simple spaghetti—you can't go wrong!

Extra-virgin olive oil, for greasing

1 pound spicy Italian sausage, casings removed

1 pound lean ground beef

½ cup panko breadcrumbs

½ cup freshly grated Parmesan cheese

2 large eggs

2 small shallots, finely chopped or grated

2 to 4 tablespoons chili paste (I like gochujang, Thai red curry paste, or crushed Calabrian chile peppers)

1 to 2 tablespoons chopped pepperoncini

Fine pink Himalayan salt and freshly ground black pepper

2 (32-ounce) jars marinara sauce (I like Rao's)

1 cup shredded mozzarella cheese

1 cup shredded provolone cheese

Fresh oregano leaves, for serving

Chopped fresh basil, for serving

1. Preheat the oven to 450°F. Grease an oven-safe baking dish or rimmed baking sheet with olive oil.

2. In a large bowl, combine the sausage, ground beef, panko, Parmesan, eggs, shallots, 1 to 2 tablespoons of the chili paste, the pepperoncini, and a pinch each of salt and pepper. Coat your hands with olive oil, then use them to combine the meat mixture. Roll the meat into spheres roughly the size of a golf ball, dividing evenly (you should have about 32), and place them in the prepared dish.

3. Bake until the meatballs are crisp on the outside, but not yet cooked through, about 15 minutes.

4. Meanwhile, in a large bowl (preferably one with a spout), stir together the marinara sauce and the remaining 2 tablespoons chili paste until smooth.

5. Remove the meatballs from the oven and carefully pour the marinara mixture over the top. Cover the pan with foil and bake for another 5 minutes. Remove the foil and add the mozzarella and provolone. Bake, uncovered, until the meatballs are cooked through and the cheese is melted and golden, about 10 minutes more.

6. Serve family style topped with fresh oregano and basil.

sesame beef bowls
with ginger tahini dressing

PREP TIME 25 minutes · COOK TIME 15 minutes · TOTAL TIME 40 minutes · SERVES 4

When my family is not asking for tacos, they are asking for any kind of Asian-inspired rice bowl. My sister is especially into them and is always requesting sesame beef bowls. And she LOVES the sauce on this steak—tahini is a great sub for the sesame paste that is popular in Chinese cooking. This sauce has just the right amount of spice, sweetness, and tang. Sesame seeds and a touch of tamari make those little frozen edamame beans absolutely irresistible. Don't skip dipping each piece of beef in the tahini sauce. I like it even better than spicy mayo!

Ginger Tahini Dressing

$1/2$ cup tahini

3 tablespoons tamari or low-sodium soy sauce

3 tablespoons toasted sesame oil

2 tablespoons pickled sushi ginger, drained

2 tablespoons juice from the pickled sushi ginger jar

2 teaspoons orange zest, plus 2 tablespoons fresh orange juice

1 tablespoon sambal oelek

1 teaspoon maple syrup

Beef

1 tablespoon ghee or salted butter

1 pound flank steak, thinly sliced against the grain

Freshly ground black pepper

6 garlic cloves, chopped

2 shallots, thinly sliced

1 (1-inch) piece fresh ginger, finely chopped or grated

$1/4$ cup plus 1 teaspoon tamari or low-sodium soy sauce

1 tablespoon sambal oelek

2 teaspoons maple syrup

1 (12-ounce) bag frozen shelled edamame, thawed

2 green onions, thinly sliced

2 tablespoons sesame seeds

2 tablespoons toasted sesame oil

Cooked rice, for serving

1. Make the dressing. In a blender or food processor, combine the tahini, tamari, sesame oil, pickled ginger, pickled ginger juice, orange zest and juice, sambal oelek, and maple syrup. Blend on high until smooth, about 30 seconds.

2. Make the beef. Melt the ghee in a large skillet over medium-high heat. Add the beef, season with black pepper, and cook, stirring, until browned, 6 to 8 minutes. Add the garlic, shallots, and ginger and cook until fragrant, 1 minute more. Reduce the heat to medium-low and add $1/4$ cup of the tamari, the sambal oelek, and maple syrup. Bring to a simmer and cook until the sauce thickens enough to nicely coat the beef, 2 to 3 minutes. Remove from the heat.

3. In a medium bowl, toss together the edamame, green onions, sesame seeds, sesame oil, and the remaining 1 teaspoon tamari.

4. Divide the rice and beef among four serving bowls. Top with the edamame mixture and drizzle lightly with ginger tahini dressing. Serve extra dressing alongside.

smothered garlic parmesan salisbury steak

PREP TIME 20 minutes · **COOK TIME** 25 minutes · **TOTAL TIME** 45 minutes · **SERVES** 4

If there is a single recipe in the book that is SO Creighton, it's this one. He's been asking for Salisbury steak for years—YEARS! I dragged my feet for ages, but when I finally made it, I will say, I did love it. (No one could love it as much as Creighton, though!) I make my version with an herbed garlic butter that you simply cannot skip. It really elevates an otherwise unfancy (but very delicious) recipe. I love to serve it with french fries and crusty bread, plus a side salad or steamed broccoli. You need something green to go with it. So good!

1 pound lean ground beef

1/2 cup panko breadcrumbs

2 tablespoons ketchup

1 large egg

1 teaspoon garlic powder

1 teaspoon onion powder

Fine pink Himalayan salt and freshly ground black pepper

3 tablespoons salted butter

8 ounces sliced cremini mushrooms

2 shallots, chopped

2 tablespoons all-purpose flour

1 cup dry white wine, such as pinot grigio or sauvignon blanc

2 cups low-sodium beef broth

1/3 cup heavy cream

1/3 cup freshly grated Parmesan cheese

2 teaspoons Dijon mustard

Roasted potatoes and/or crusty bread, for serving

Herbed Garlic Butter

1/2 cup chopped fresh herbs, such as thyme, sage, and/or parsley

2 tablespoons salted butter, at room temperature

1 garlic clove, finely chopped or grated

Freshly ground black pepper (optional)

1. In a large bowl, combine the ground beef, panko, ketchup, egg, garlic powder, and onion powder, and season with salt and pepper. Using your hands, mix well to incorporate all the ingredients. Divide the meat into four equal balls and pat each into an oval-shaped patty, about 3/4 inch thick. You want them to be on the thin side.

2. Melt 1 tablespoon of the butter in a large skillet over medium-high heat. Add the patties and cook until browned on the bottom, about 2 minutes. Flip and cook until browned all over, another minute. Transfer the patties to a plate.

3. Melt 1 tablespoon butter in the same skillet (no need to wipe it out) over medium-high heat. Add the mushrooms and shallots and cook, stirring often, until the shallots are softened and the mushrooms caramelized, 4 to 5 minutes.

4. Stir in the flour and remaining 1 tablespoon butter and cook until incorporated, about 1 minute. Whisk in the wine and cook until it is reduced by about half, 3 to 4 minutes. Add the broth and cook until it is again reduced by half, 5 to 6 minutes more. Add the cream, Parmesan, and mustard and whisk until incorporated, about 1 minute.

5. Reduce the heat to medium-low. Slide the patties back into the skillet along with any collected juices and spoon the sauce and mushrooms over the steaks. Cook until the sauce thickens around the patties, 5 to 8 minutes.

6. Meanwhile, make the garlic butter. In a small bowl, stir together the herbs, butter, and garlic. Season with pepper, if desired.

7. Plate the Salisbury steaks and top with the mushroom gravy. Spoon the sauce over the steaks and serve with garlic butter and potatoes or bread for soaking up the sauce.

honey balsamic short ribs

PREP TIME 15 minutes · **COOK TIME** See specific method · **SERVES** 6

Yes, you've probably seen plenty of short rib recipes, cooked in wine and served over potatoes. But I love cooking short ribs in unusual ways—they're so versatile! This balsamic sauce is the one my Nonnie would use to cook her honey balsamic chicken. It's so simple that no searing is needed on the meat. I love these ribs over rice with a side of sesame asparagus or broccoli.

6 bone-in beef short ribs, each about 12 ounces (about 4½ pounds total)

Fine pink Himalayan salt and freshly ground black pepper

4 shallots, halved

4 garlic cloves, chopped

2 tablespoons fresh thyme leaves

1 tablespoon fresh oregano leaves

Crushed red pepper flakes

1 cup balsamic vinegar

1 cup red wine, pomegranate juice, or low-sodium beef broth

½ cup honey

1 cup crumbled feta cheese

½ cup toasted pine nuts

¼ cup chopped fresh dill

¼ cup fresh lemon juice

Cooked rice, for serving

OVEN
COOK TIME: 3 hours

1. Preheat the oven to 325°F.

2. Season the short ribs all over with salt and pepper and place them in a large, oven-safe braiser or Dutch oven. Add the shallots, garlic, thyme, and oregano and season with red pepper flakes. Pour over the balsamic, wine, honey, and 2 cups water.

3. Cover and bake for about 2½ hours, then carefully remove the lid and continue baking until the short ribs are tender and falling off the bone and the sauce has mostly reduced, about 30 minutes more.

4. Remove from the oven and use a skimmer or spoon to remove and discard excess fat from the sauce. Use tongs or two forks to shred the meat, discarding the bones. Toss the meat into the sauce to coat well.

5. Meanwhile, in a medium bowl, combine the feta, pine nuts, dill, and lemon juice. Stir to mix well.

6. To serve, spoon the shredded meat and sauce over rice and top with the feta mixture.

SLOW COOKER
COOK TIME: 4 to 8 hours

1. Season the short ribs with salt and pepper and place them in the bowl of a slow cooker. Add the shallots, garlic, thyme, and oregano and season with red pepper flakes. Pour over the balsamic, wine, honey, and ¼ cup water.

2. Cover and cook on low for 6 to 8 hours or on high for 4 to 6 hours, removing the lid during the final hour of cooking.

3. Finish and serve as directed in steps 4 through 6 for the oven.

fish & seafood

sheet pan lemon shrimp

PREP TIME 15 minutes · COOK TIME 15 minutes · TOTAL TIME 30 minutes · SERVES 6

Everyone makes lemon shrimp—and it's easy to see why, since the two ingredients go together so well. But instead of making it as usual in a skillet, I like to roast it on a sheet pan. It cooks perfectly every single time and is even easier this way! The lemon sauce comes together with a touch of honey, which really makes the shrimp extra delish. I love this over rice for dinner with some fresh herbs on top, but it's great as an appetizer, too. I always serve this with sesame seeds on top for a little nutty crunch!

2 pounds large raw tail-on shrimp, peeled and deveined

4 tablespoons extra-virgin olive oil

3 tablespoons all-purpose flour

2 tablespoons lemon zest

Fine pink Himalayan salt and freshly ground black pepper

4 cups broccoli florets (from 1 medium head)

Thinly sliced green onions, for serving

Sesame seeds, for serving

Lemon Sauce

⅓ cup tamari or low-sodium soy sauce

¼ cup fresh lemon juice

1 tablespoon honey

2 tablespoons rice vinegar

1 tablespoon toasted sesame oil

4 garlic cloves, finely chopped or grated

1 (1-inch) piece fresh ginger, grated

1 to 2 teaspoons crushed red pepper flakes

1 teaspoon cornstarch or all-purpose flour

1. Preheat the oven to 450°F. Line a baking sheet with parchment paper.

2. On the prepared sheet pan, toss together the shrimp, 2 tablespoons of olive oil, the flour, lemon zest, and pepper. Arrange the shrimp in a single layer on one half of the baking sheet. Add the broccoli to the empty half and toss with the remaining 2 tablespoons olive oil, salt, and pepper. Arrange in an even layer.

3. Bake until the shrimp is pink, opaque, and cooked through, about 8 minutes.

4. Meanwhile, make the lemon sauce. In a small pan, combine the tamari, lemon juice, honey, rice vinegar, sesame oil, garlic, ginger, red pepper flakes, and cornstarch. Place over medium heat and bring to a boil. Cook, stirring, until the sauce bubbles and begins to thicken, 3 to 4 minutes. Remove from the heat.

5. Pour the lemon sauce over the shrimp and broccoli and toss to coat. Bake until the sauce thickens around the shrimp and broccoli, 4 to 5 minutes more.

6. To serve, transfer the shrimp and broccoli to a platter and spoon over any remaining sauce from the pan. Garnish with green onions and sesame seeds.

fish tacos
with jalapeño cream & avocado salsa

PREP TIME 20 minutes · COOK TIME 10 minutes · TOTAL TIME 30 minutes · SERVES 4 to 6

We love ALL tacos, but my dad and my brother Brendan always prefer a fish taco to the beef ones I'm usually making. Any time I get the chance to feed Bren, I make these. They are his favorite fish taco ever, he says. He lives in California, where fish tacos are plentiful, so that feels like a pretty big accomplishment for me! What he loves most is the seasoning blend on the fish, then all the toppings—a bit of homemade jalapeño cream and quick avocado salsa, too. In spring and summer, I switch up the salsa and add mango chunks, which always make the tacos feel and taste just a little bit more tropical!

2 pounds boneless, skinless white fish, such as tilapia, cod, or mahi mahi, cut into cubes

3 tablespoons extra-virgin olive oil

1 tablespoon all-purpose flour

2 teaspoons smoked paprika

2 teaspoons chipotle chile powder

1 teaspoon garlic powder

1 teaspoon onion powder

Fine pink Himalayan salt

$1/2$ cup hot sauce (I like Frank's RedHot)

6 tablespoons ($3/4$ stick) salted butter, melted

12 corn tortillas

Jalapeño Cream

1 cup sour cream or plain Greek yogurt

$3/4$ cup fresh cilantro, chopped

$1/3$ cup fresh lime juice

$1/4$ cup chopped pickled jalapeños

1 teaspoon garlic powder

1 teaspoon onion powder

Fine pink Himalayan salt

Avocado Salsa

2 avocados, diced

$1/2$ cup cilantro, chopped

$1/4$ cup chopped green onions

Juice of 1 lime

1 jalapeño, seeded if desired, and chopped

Fine pink Himalayan salt

1. Preheat the oven to 450°F.

2. On a baking sheet, combine the fish pieces with the olive oil, flour, paprika, chipotle chile powder, garlic powder, onion powder, and salt. Toss to coat well. Bake until the fish is cooked through and flakes easily, about 8 minutes. Turn the oven to broil and cook until lightly charred, 2 to 3 minutes.

3. In a small bowl, stir together the hot sauce and butter. Drizzle several spoonfuls of the sauce over the fish, reserving the remainder for serving.

4. Make the jalapeño cream. In a medium bowl, combine the sour cream, cilantro, lime juice, pickled jalapeños, garlic powder, and onion powder. Season with salt and stir to mix well.

5. Make the salsa. In a small bowl, combine the avocados, cilantro, green onions, lime juice, and jalapeño. Season with salt and gently toss to combine.

6. Warm the tortillas (you can lay them out directly on the oven rack for about 30 seconds, or microwave them). To serve, spoon the salsa into the warm tortillas and top with the fish, reserved butter sauce, and jalapeño cream.

tilapia in wine sauce
with mushrooms & crispy prosciutto

PREP TIME 15 minutes · **COOK TIME** 25 minutes · **TOTAL TIME** 40 minutes · **SERVES** 6

If you've ever felt bored by tilapia, or any other white fish, this recipe will totally change your mind. The sauce, the mushrooms, the crispy prosciutto! None of those are necessarily served with such a delicate piece of seafood traditionally, but that doesn't mean we can't give it a go. Trust me—tilapia smothered in cream sauce is delicious! I recommend crusty bread for scooping it all up, of course. And the crispy prosciutto makes this dish shine and feel a little more special.

6 (5-ounce) tilapia fillets

1 teaspoon garlic powder

1 teaspoon smoked paprika

Fine pink Himalayan salt and freshly ground black pepper

3 ounces thinly sliced prosciutto, torn

4 tablespoons (½ stick) salted butter

8 ounces sliced cremini or shiitake mushrooms

1 lemon, sliced, plus wedges, for serving

4 garlic cloves, chopped

2 tablespoons fresh thyme leaves

1 cup dry white wine, such as pinot grigio or sauvignon blanc

Chopped fresh dill, for serving

Crusty bread, for serving

1. Preheat the oven to 400°F.

2. Season the tilapia all over with the garlic powder, paprika, and salt and pepper.

3. In a large skillet set over medium-low heat, arrange the prosciutto. Cook, undisturbed, until crispy all over, 4 to 5 minutes. Transfer the prosciutto to a small plate.

4. In the same skillet over medium heat, melt 1 tablespoon of the butter. Add the mushrooms and cook, undisturbed, until golden on the bottom, 5 to 7 minutes. Add the remaining 3 tablespoons butter, the lemon slices, garlic, thyme, and a pinch each of salt and pepper. Cook, stirring, until the butter is melted and everything is coated and fragrant, 1 to 2 minutes more.

5. Pour in the wine, then remove the skillet from the heat and gently slide the tilapia into the sauce. Bake until the fish is opaque and flakes easily, 10 to 12 minutes.

6. Top with crispy prosciutto and dill. Serve the tilapia with lemon wedges for squeezing and crusty bread for mopping up all that delicious sauce.

red curry salmon
with avocado-cucumber salad & coconut rice

PREP TIME 20 minutes · COOK TIME 25 minutes · TOTAL TIME 50 minutes · SERVES 4

I love making salmon and rice together, and I probably do it once a week on average. I almost never do it the same way twice, but I do usually keep the seasoning on the salmon the same because it is so good! This mix of Thai red curry paste, tamari, and honey is spicy, salty, and sweet—the mix of flavors everyone seems to enjoy most. The coconut rice here is just the perfect complement, creamy with a nice subtle flavor. Add that avocado salad and YUM!

Coconut Rice

1 (14-ounce) can unsweetened full-fat coconut milk

¾ cup low-sodium chicken broth

2 tablespoons ghee or salted butter

2 cups jasmine rice

Fine pink Himalayan salt

Salmon

5 tablespoons extra-virgin olive oil

1 teaspoon chipotle chile powder

¼ cup Thai red curry paste

1 tablespoon tamari or low-sodium soy sauce

2 teaspoons honey

4 (4- to 6-ounce) salmon fillets

3 tablespoons salted butter, sliced

Avocado-Cucumber Salad

2 avocados, diced

2 small Persian cucumbers, chopped

½ cup fresh cilantro or Thai basil, chopped

¼ cup sesame seeds

¼ cup chopped peanuts

2 green onions, thinly sliced

1 serrano or jalapeño, seeded if desired, sliced

2 tablespoons fresh lime juice

Fine pink Himalayan salt

1. Place a rack in the top third of the oven and preheat to 450°F.

2. Make the rice. In a medium pot, combine the coconut milk, broth, and ghee. Bring to a low boil over medium-high heat. Add the rice and a pinch of salt. Stir to combine, cover, then reduce the heat to low. Cook for 10 minutes, then turn the heat off completely. Let the rice sit, still covered, for another 20 minutes (don't peek!). Remove the lid and fluff the rice with a fork.

3. Meanwhile, make the salmon. In a small bowl, stir together 3 tablespoons of the olive oil, the chipotle chile powder, curry paste, tamari, and honey. Arrange the salmon on a baking sheet. Rub the mixture over each fillet and dot with the butter.

4. Bake until the salmon is warm in the center and turning opaque, 8 to 10 minutes, or longer to your liking. Turn on the broiler and cook until the curry mixture is lightly charred, 2 to 3 minutes more.

5. Meanwhile, make the salad. In a medium bowl, combine the avocados, cucumbers, cilantro, sesame seeds, peanuts, green onions, and serrano. Add the remaining 2 tablespoons olive oil and the lime juice and season with salt. Gently toss to mix well.

6. To serve, divide the coconut rice among plates. Add the salmon and top with the salad.

brown butter scallops
with candied bacon

PREP TIME 15 minutes · **COOK TIME** 15 minutes · **TOTAL TIME** 30 minutes · **SERVES** 4

Anytime I make scallops, it feels like a special occasion. They are just so luxurious! Especially the way I cook them, which is almost always in a brown butter sauce with bacon. Sometimes, I just can't make scallops any other way! My only other suggestion for this recipe is to add fries on the side. I don't know what it is, but I think homemade oven fries are just delish here. And trust me: No one ever complains about a side of fries!

6 to 8 slices thick-cut bacon, chopped

1 tablespoon chopped fresh rosemary

1 teaspoon honey

1/2 teaspoon cayenne pepper

1 1/2 pounds large sea scallops (15 to 20 scallops)

Fine pink Himalayan salt and freshly ground black pepper

2 tablespoons extra-virgin olive oil

4 tablespoons (1/2 stick) salted butter

1/4 cup fresh lemon juice

4 to 6 garlic cloves, smashed

6 sprigs fresh herbs (such as thyme or sage)

Crushed red pepper flakes

Crusty bread, for serving (optional)

1. Preheat the oven to 400°F. Line a baking sheet with parchment paper.

2. On the prepared baking sheet, toss together the bacon, rosemary, honey, and cayenne. Spread in an even layer and bake until the bacon is crisp, 10 to 12 minutes.

3. Meanwhile, pat the scallops dry and season with salt and pepper.

4. In a large skillet over medium heat, heat the olive oil. When the oil is shimmering, add the scallops and sear until browned, 3 to 4 minutes, then flip. Add the butter, lemon juice, garlic, and herbs, and season with red pepper flakes. Cook, scraping up any browned bits from the bottom of the pan and spooning the butter over the scallops, until the garlic is fragrant and the scallops are opaque and cooked through, 3 to 4 minutes more.

5. Spoon the scallops and sauce onto plates and top with the candied bacon. Serve with crusty bread for soaking up the delicious sauce.

creamed spinach salmon
with lemony herbs

PREP TIME 10 minutes · **COOK TIME** 15 minutes · **TOTAL TIME** 25 minutes · **SERVES** 4

I make this salmon all year long—it's a staple in my kitchen. The lemony garlic cream sauce tastes wonderful, and baking the salmon (versus pan-frying it) is totally fuss-free. I actually took this recipe from my mom. When my brothers and I were younger, she would make chicken Florentine on special occasions or Sunday nights. The spinach and Parmesan cream sauce around the chicken was, of course, the best part. All I did was use her sauce recipe, add fresh lemon to it, and replace the chicken with salmon. I think the salmon is even more delicious! I love to top this dish with fresh herbs like basil, parsley, thyme, or dill for a pop of color just before serving. I serve it straight from the skillet—it's easy and looks so pretty, too!

4 (6-ounce) salmon fillets

Fine pink Himalayan salt and freshly ground black pepper

4 tablespoons salted butter

2 tablespoons extra-virgin olive oil

1 shallot, thinly sliced

3 garlic cloves, chopped

Crushed red pepper flakes

1 cup heavy cream

1 tablespoon Dijon mustard

5 ounces fresh baby spinach

1/2 cup freshly grated Parmesan cheese

1/4 cup fresh basil, chopped

1/4 cup fresh parsley, chopped

1 tablespoon fresh thyme leaves

Zest and juice of 1 lemon

Flaky sea salt, for serving

1. Place a rack in the top third of the oven and preheat to 425°F.

2. Season the salmon with salt and pepper.

3. In a large high-sided ovenproof skillet over medium-high heat, melt 1 tablespoon of the butter with the olive oil. Add the shallot and garlic and cook, stirring, until the garlic is very fragrant, about 2 minutes. Season with red pepper flakes.

4. Reduce the heat to medium and stir in the cream and mustard. Bring to a simmer, stirring constantly, until the sauce thickens slightly, 1 to 2 minutes. Season with salt and pepper. Add the spinach and Parmesan and cook until the spinach is wilted, 1 to 2 minutes. Remove the pan from the heat and slide the salmon into the sauce. Slice the remaining 3 tablespoons butter and scatter it over the top of the salmon.

5. Bake until the salmon is warm in the center and turning opaque, 8 to 10 minutes, or longer to your liking. During the last 4 minutes, turn on the broiler to brown the top of the salmon.

6. In a small bowl, combine the basil, parsley, thyme, and lemon zest and juice. Toss to combine. Spoon the cream sauce over the salmon in the skillet. Top with the herb mixture and finish with flaky salt before serving.

sweet thai chili fish burgers

PREP TIME 20 minutes · **COOK TIME** 10 minutes · **TOTAL TIME** 30 minutes · **SERVES** 4

If I am going to make a burger of any kind, it's going to be a REALLY delicious burger—otherwise it's just not worth doing! This fish burger is both really delicious and really easy, and you can make it any time of year. My shortcut is using tinned fish, which I think is an undervalued ingredient. I always have canned salmon, tuna, and sardines in my pantry and I cook with them all the time. Typically I use canned salmon in this recipe, but tuna is delicious, too—use whatever you like. And the toppings! A burger without toppings is sad, so I pile mine with fresh herbs tossed with lime juice and sesame seeds, pickled ginger, and that sweet chili mayo. Honestly, the mayo is all you need. It makes you say "yummy" with every single bite—I usually double the recipe.

Burgers

1 (14.75-ounce) can tinned fish, such as salmon or tuna, well drained

½ cup panko breadcrumbs

2 large eggs

2 tablespoons sweet Thai chili sauce

2 tablespoons chopped pickled sushi ginger

2 teaspoons fish sauce, tamari, or low-sodium soy sauce

4 green onions, thinly sliced

Freshly ground black pepper

2 tablespoons avocado or extra-virgin olive oil, for cooking

½ cup fresh loosely packed Thai basil, chopped

½ cup fresh cilantro, chopped

2 tablespoons fresh lime juice

1 tablespoon sesame seeds

Fine pink Himalayan salt

4 burger buns, toasted

Sweet Chili Mayo

½ cup mayonnaise

2 tablespoons sweet Thai chili sauce

1 tablespoon fresh lime juice

½ teaspoon smoked or sweet paprika

1. Make the burgers. In a medium bowl, combine the fish, panko, eggs, chili sauce, ginger, fish sauce, and half of the green onions. Season with pepper. Use your hands to mix well, then form into 4 patties.

2. In a large skillet over medium heat, heat the oil. When the oil is shimmering, add the burgers and cook, turning once, until browned and cooked through, 3 to 5 minutes per side.

3. Meanwhile, in a separate medium bowl, stir together the basil, cilantro, the remaining green onions, the lime juice, and sesame seeds. Season with salt.

4. Make the sweet chili mayo. In medium bowl, combine the mayo, chili sauce, lime juice, and paprika. Stir to mix well.

5. To assemble, slather the insides of the toasted buns with chili mayo. Add the burgers to the bottom halves and top with the herb mixture. Finish with the top halves of the buns and enjoy with extra chili mayo alongside.

southern garlic shrimp
with bacon–sweet corn polenta

PREP TIME 25 minutes · COOK TIME 25 minutes · TOTAL TIME 50 minutes · SERVES 6

When it comes to Southern cooking, grits are pretty traditional, and they're served with many dishes, from a savory breakfast to a chicken or seafood dinner. I love them! What I don't love is how they can be a little time intensive to make, so instead of grits I often use polenta, which is milled more finely and therefore cooks faster. The polenta gets this Southern-inspired dinner on the table much faster, and it's just as creamy and delicious as the classic. The bacon and corn combo adds smoky, salty, and sweet flavors. This is the perfect summertime meal, when you really want a cozier dinner but still something quick and summery. The buttery shrimp always hits the spot!

Polenta

4 slices thick-cut bacon, chopped

2 tablespoons salted butter

3 cups fresh or frozen corn kernels (from 3 ears of corn)

2 cups milk of your choice

1 cup instant or quick-cooking polenta

Fine pink Himalayan salt and freshly ground black pepper

Shrimp

2 tablespoons extra-virgin olive oil

6 tablespoons (¾ stick) salted butter

1½ pounds jumbo raw tail-on shrimp, peeled and deveined

1 tablespoon Homemade Cajun Seasoning (recipe follows) or store-bought Cajun seasoning

Freshly ground black pepper

3 garlic cloves, chopped

2 tablespoons fresh thyme leaves

1 tablespoon fresh lemon juice

Fresh basil leaves, for serving

1. Make the polenta. In a medium pan, cook the bacon over high heat until it begins to crisp and has rendered its fat, 7 to 8 minutes. Using a slotted spoon, transfer the bacon to a paper towel–lined plate. Drain all but 1 tablespoon of bacon fat from the pan.

2. Melt the butter in the same pan over medium heat. Add the corn and cook, stirring occasionally, until the butter browns around the corn, 6 to 8 minutes. Add the milk and 2 cups water. Bring to a gentle boil, then slowly whisk in the polenta. Cook, stirring often, until the polenta softens and thickens, about 5 minutes. Turn off the heat, cover the pot, and let the polenta sit for 5 minutes until all the liquid is absorbed. Season with salt and pepper and stir in the bacon.

3. Meanwhile, make the shrimp. In a large skillet over medium heat, heat the olive oil. When the oil is shimmering, add the butter, shrimp, Cajun seasoning, and a big pinch of pepper. Cook until the shrimp is pink and opaque, 2 to 3 minutes per side. Stir in the garlic and thyme and continue to cook until the garlic is fragrant, 1 minute more. Remove the pan from the heat and stir in the lemon juice.

4. To serve, divide the polenta among bowls, spoon the shrimp and sauce over the top, then finish with basil leaves.

homemade cajun seasoning

MAKES ¾ CUP

3 tablespoons smoked paprika

2 tablespoons garlic powder

1½ tablespoons fine pink Himalayan salt

1 tablespoon onion powder

1 tablespoon dried oregano

1 tablespoon dried thyme

1 tablespoon chili powder

1 tablespoon cayenne pepper

1 tablespoon freshly ground black pepper

In a glass jar, combine the paprika, garlic powder, salt, onion powder, oregano, thyme, chili powder, cayenne, and black pepper. Stir well to combine, then seal and store in a cool, dark place for up to 6 months.

crunchy fish bites
with pickled mayo

PREP TIME 15 minutes · COOK TIME 15 minutes · TOTAL TIME 30 minutes · SERVES 6

Like many, I grew up eating frozen chicken fingers. What I did not grow up with was fish—not even frozen fish sticks! My mom has never been into seafood, so she just would not buy fish sticks. But during one of my first visits with my Nonnie in Florida, we both ordered the battered and fried fish sticks for lunch. And, dang it, they were delicious. Honestly, they tasted like chicken fingers! And the pickled mayo they came with for dipping was special. I remember it so well! And now I have my own recipe for it. These fish bites are great because instead of fussing around with frying, you bake them up—so easy! And, yes, I have found that kids definitely love these, especially when served with french fries!

Fish Bites

6 cups cornflakes

1/4 cup freshly grated Parmesan cheese

1 teaspoon smoked paprika

1 teaspoon chipotle chile powder or chili powder

1/2 teaspoon onion powder

1/2 teaspoon garlic powder

Fine pink Himalayan salt

2 large eggs

2 pounds skinless fish fillets, such as salmon, tilapia, or mahi mahi, cut into bite-size pieces

Extra-virgin olive oil, for brushing

Lemon and lime wedges, for serving

Pickled Mayo

1/2 cup mayonnaise

2 tablespoons finely chopped dill pickles

2 tablespoons dill pickle juice

2 teaspoons honey

Fine pink Himalayan salt

1. Preheat the oven to 425°F. Line a baking sheet with parchment paper.

2. Make the fish bites. In a food processor, combine the cornflakes, Parmesan, paprika, chipotle chile powder, onion powder, garlic powder, and a pinch of salt. Pulse into fine crumbs, about 15 seconds. Transfer the crumbs to a shallow bowl.

3. In a separate shallow bowl, beat the eggs. Add the fish pieces to the eggs, and gently turn to coat, allowing excess to drip off. Dredge the fish through the crumbs, pressing to adhere. Place on the prepared baking sheet and brush lightly with olive oil.

4. Bake until the coating is crisp and the fish is cooked through, 15 to 20 minutes.

5. Meanwhile, make the pickled mayo. In a small bowl, combine the mayo, pickles, pickle juice, and honey. Season with salt and stir to combine.

6. Transfer the fish bites to a serving platter. Just before serving, drizzle with the warm hot honey. Serve with the pickled mayo on the side for dipping and lemon wedges for squeezing.

honey mustard salmon bowls
with avocado-feta herb salad

PREP TIME 20 minutes · **COOK TIME** 10 minutes · **TOTAL TIME** 30 minutes · **SERVES 6**

My brother Creighton LOVES honey mustard. Until he asked me to make it for him, I hadn't ever tried it, but now I love it, too. My favorite way to use it is to dip warm, soft pretzels in that creamy, spicy sauce. SO yummy. If we're talking about making honey mustard the star of a meal, pairing it with chicken or putting it on a salad is popular, but I think it's even more delicious with salmon. I love to cut my salmon into bite-size pieces and coat them completely in the mustard so they get a little crispy and caramelized. Rice and a simple salad are the perfect accompaniments—but you MUST do each bowl up with lots of extra honey mustard sauce. It's the only way!

¹⁄₃ cup Dijon mustard	**Avocado-Feta Herb Salad**	**Honey Mustard Sauce**
¹⁄₄ cup honey	2 avocados, chopped	¹⁄₄ cup grainy Dijon mustard
4 garlic cloves, chopped	¹⁄₂ cup crumbled feta cheese	3 tablespoons mayonnaise
2 teaspoons onion powder	¹⁄₂ cup fresh cilantro and/or basil, chopped	3 tablespoons honey
1 teaspoon smoked paprika		2 tablespoons fresh lemon juice
¹⁄₂ teaspoon chili powder	2 green onions, thinly sliced	2 tablespoons apple cider vinegar
Fine pink Himalayan salt and freshly ground pepper	1 serrano or jalapeño, seeded if desired, sliced	Fine pink Himalayan salt and freshly ground black pepper
2 pounds salmon fillets, cut into pieces	2 tablespoons extra-virgin olive oil	
2 tablespoons extra-virgin olive oil	1 tablespoon fresh lemon juice	
3 to 4 cups cooked basmati rice	1 tablespoon fresh lime juice	
	Fine pink Himalayan salt	

1. Place a rack in the top third of the oven and preheat to 450°F.

2. In a small bowl, stir together the mustard, honey, garlic, onion powder, paprika, and chili powder. Season with salt and pepper. Place the salmon on a baking sheet. Rub with the mustard mixture, then drizzle with the olive oil.

3. Bake until the salmon is warm in the center and turning opaque, 8 to 10 minutes, or longer to your liking. For the last 1 to 2 minutes, turn the oven to broil and broil until the salmon is browned on top.

4. Meanwhile, make the salad. In a medium bowl, combine the avocados, feta, cilantro, green onions, and serrano. Add the olive oil, lemon juice, and lime juice and toss gently to mix. Season with salt.

5. Make the honey mustard sauce. In a medium bowl, combine the grainy Dijon, mayo, honey, lemon juice, and vinegar. Season with salt and pepper and whisk to combine.

6. Divide the rice among bowls and add the salmon. Top with the avocado salad and spoon the honey mustard sauce on top.

lemon butter cod
with mediterranean orzo

PREP TIME 15 minutes · **COOK TIME** 30 minutes · **TOTAL TIME** 45 minutes · **SERVES** 6

Some of my most reliable go-to dishes are the ones I have made using just one skillet. Most of the time, it's chicken and orzo or chicken and rice. But when I'm looking for a seafood dinner, I just love making this skillet cod. The fish melts into the buttery, herby orzo and it comes out wonderful every time. Make this in the spring or summer, when fresh herbs are plentiful. Bread on the side is a must, too!

6 (4- to 6-ounce) cod fillets

Fine pink Himalayan salt and freshly ground black pepper

¼ cup freshly grated Parmesan cheese

2 tablespoons all-purpose flour

2 tablespoons fresh thyme leaves, plus more for serving

1 teaspoon smoked paprika

¼ teaspoon cayenne pepper

3 tablespoons salted butter

1 tablespoon extra-virgin olive oil, plus more as needed

1 shallot, chopped

6 garlic cloves, chopped

2 tablespoons pine nuts

1 tablespoon chopped fresh sage

Crushed red pepper flakes

1 cup dry white wine, such as pinot grigio or sauvignon blanc

1 cup low-sodium chicken broth, plus more as needed

¾ cup orzo pasta or pearl couscous

½ cup smashed pitted green olives

¼ cup fresh lemon juice

1. Pat the cod dry and season all over with salt and pepper. In a shallow bowl, combine the Parmesan, flour, 1 tablespoon of thyme, the paprika, and cayenne. Dredge the cod through the flour mixture, turning to coat and pressing to adhere.

2. In a large skillet over medium heat, melt 1 tablespoon of the butter with the olive oil. Working in batches, add the cod and cook, turning once, until golden, about 3 minutes per side, adding more oil as needed. When all the cod fillets have been cooked, return them to the pan. Add 1 tablespoon of butter, swirling the pan so the butter browns around the fish, about 2 minutes. Carefully transfer the fish to a plate.

3. In the same skillet, melt the remaining 1 tablespoon butter. Add the shallot, garlic, pine nuts, sage, and remaining 1 tablespoon thyme. Season with salt, black pepper, and red pepper flakes. Cook, stirring, until fragrant, about 2 minutes. Add the wine and cook until the liquid is reduced by about half, 2 minutes. Pour in the broth, then stir in the orzo and olives. Simmer, stirring occasionally, until the orzo is just shy of al dente, about 10 minutes, adding more broth as needed. Slide the cod back into the skillet. Add the lemon juice and cook just until the mixture is simmering, 1 to 2 minutes. Remove the skillet from the heat.

4. To serve, divide the cod and orzo among plates and sprinkle lightly with thyme.

sheet pan mahi mahi & baby potatoes
with feta-olive dressing

PREP TIME 25 minutes · **COOK TIME** 30 minutes · **TOTAL TIME** 55 minutes · **SERVES** 4 to 6

This fish is SO DELICIOUS—my dad even told me it might be one of his favorite recipes . . . ever! There is so much flavor in this dish, and you know everything tastes just a little bit better when it's cooked in just one pan. And I just adore this salty feta and olive dressing. It's not a topping you might expect to see paired with fish, but it really elevates an otherwise simple sheet pan fish dinner—something special to finish it off! If you are having trouble finding mahi mahi, try using swordfish, cod, or tilapia.

1 pound baby yellow potatoes, halved

2 tablespoons plus ½ cup extra-virgin olive oil

Fine pink Himalayan salt and freshly ground black pepper

2 tablespoons balsamic vinegar

1 shallot, chopped

4 garlic cloves, chopped

1 tablespoon lemon zest

2 teaspoons dried oregano

½ teaspoon chipotle chile powder

Crushed red pepper flakes

4 to 6 (6- to 8-ounce) mahi mahi fillets

1 to 2 red bell peppers, thinly sliced

2 tablespoons sesame seeds

Feta-Olive Dressing

2 cups mixed fresh tender herbs, such as parsley, basil, dill, and/or thyme, chopped

6 to 8 ounces feta cheese, cubed

¾ cup pitted Castelvetrano olives, roughly chopped

1 to 2 pepperoncini, finely chopped

¼ cup extra-virgin olive oil

2 tablespoons fresh lemon juice

1. Preheat the oven to 425°F.

2. On a baking sheet, toss the potatoes with 2 tablespoons of the olive oil. Season with salt and pepper. Bake until they are knife-tender and lightly browned, about 20 minutes.

3. Meanwhile, in a large, shallow bowl, combine the remaining ½ cup olive oil, the balsamic, shallot, garlic, lemon zest, oregano, and chipotle chile powder. Season with salt, black pepper, and red pepper flakes. Add the mahi mahi fillets. Set aside to marinate while the potatoes cook, stirring around a few times so all the fish is nicely coated.

4. Remove the potatoes from the oven. Add the bell pepper, season with salt and pepper, and carefully mix in with the potatoes. Scoot the potatoes and pepper to the edges of the pan and nestle the mahi mahi in the center, skin-side up. Pour over any remaining marinade and sprinkle the sesame seeds over the top. Bake until the fish is opaque and flaky, 10 to 15 minutes.

5. Meanwhile, make the feta-olive dressing. In a medium bowl, combine the herbs, feta, olives, and pepperoncini. Stir lightly, then add the olive oil and lemon juice, mixing just to combine.

6. To serve, divide the mahi mahi, potatoes, and peppers among plates. Spoon the pan sauce over and top with the feta-olive dressing.

herby roasted cod
with caramelized squash

PREP TIME 20 minutes · **COOK TIME** 40 minutes · **TOTAL TIME** 1 hour · **SERVES** 4

My go-tos when I make seafood are usually salmon and shrimp, or if I am making fish tacos, some kind of white fish. Cod was never a fish I played around with until more recently—and now I love it. It cooks quickly and beautifully, has nice meaty flakes, and is mild enough that it takes on pretty much any flavor. In this dish, the herb sauce is so delicious, with cilantro, jalapeños, and ginger. The small amount of allspice and honey add a nice warmth and sweetness that balances it all out. I make this most in the fall and winter, when winter squashes, which I love roasting alongside the fish, are in season. If you can find it, use delicata squash. It doesn't need to be peeled, and its creaminess really makes this dish special!

Squash

1 to 2 small winter squash, such as delicata, acorn, or honeynut, quartered and seeded

6 tablespoons (¾ stick) salted butter, cubed

1 tablespoon honey

¼ teaspoon ground cinnamon

Fine pink Himalayan salt and freshly ground black pepper

Cod

½ cup fresh cilantro

2 green onions, quartered

1 to 2 jalapeños, seeded, if desired

4 garlic cloves, smashed

1 (1-inch) piece fresh ginger, chopped

1 tablespoon tomato paste

2 tablespoons fish sauce, tamari, or low-sodium soy sauce

2 teaspoons honey

¼ teaspoon ground allspice

4 tablespoons (½ stick) salted butter, melted

2 tablespoons extra-virgin olive oil

Fine pink Himalayan salt

4 (6-ounce) cod fillets

For Serving

1 cup pomegranate seeds

Fresh dill

1. Make the squash. Preheat the oven to 425°F. Line a baking sheet with parchment paper.

2. Place the squash on the prepared baking sheet, cut-side up. Dot the butter over the squash, then drizzle with the honey. Sprinkle with the cinnamon, and season with salt and pepper. Bake until golden brown and knife-tender, about 20 minutes.

3. Meanwhile, make the cod. In a food processor, combine the cilantro, green onions, jalapeño, garlic, ginger, tomato paste, fish sauce, honey, and allspice. Pulse until finely chopped, scraping down the sides as needed. Add the butter and oil and pulse until combined. Season with salt.

4. Remove the squash from the oven and carefully scoot it to the edges of the baking sheet. Arrange the cod fillets in the center. Using about half of the herb sauce, rub the fillets with the mixture, dividing evenly. Return the pan to the oven and bake until the cod is baked through, 15 to 20 minutes.

5. Meanwhile, in a small skillet over medium heat, heat the remaining herb sauce until warmed through and fragrant, 2 to 3 minutes.

6. To serve, divide the cod and squash among plates, drizzle them with the warmed herb sauce, and top with the pomegranate seeds and dill.

dessert

blueberry peach cobbler

PREP TIME 20 minutes · **COOK TIME** 1 hour · **TOTAL TIME** 1 hour 20 minutes · **SERVES** 8 to 10

This is THE most wonderful cobbler . . . or cobblers, if you want to make it in cute mini skillets like I sometimes do! I make this recipe during the summer when juicy peaches are at their peak. Blueberries or blackberries are my go-to berry alongside—their flavors are the sweetest. The one thing you must do is serve this warm, while the juices are still bubbling up and everything smells incredible. Add a scoop of your favorite vanilla ice cream or fresh whipped cream—you just can't enjoy a warm cobbler without it! This is dangerously delicious, dangerously addicting, and all-around perfection. I just know you'll love it!

2 pounds peaches,
cut into wedges

1 pound fresh blueberries

6 tablespoons ($\frac{3}{4}$ stick)
salted butter, cubed, plus
3 tablespoons, cold and sliced

1 cup packed light or
dark brown sugar

2 tablespoons maple syrup

2 teaspoons cornstarch

1 cup all-purpose flour

2 teaspoons baking powder

1 teaspoon ground cinnamon

$\frac{1}{2}$ teaspoon fine pink
Himalayan salt

$\frac{2}{3}$ cup sour cream

$\frac{1}{3}$ cup milk of your choice,
plus more as needed

1 tablespoon pure
vanilla extract

Cinnamon Spice Sugar

2 tablespoons granulated sugar

1 teaspoon ground cinnamon

$\frac{1}{8}$ teaspoon ground allspice

$\frac{1}{8}$ teaspoon ground ginger

Fine pink Himalayan salt

Vanilla ice cream or whipped
cream, for serving

1. Preheat the oven to 375°F.

2. In a 9 x 13-inch baking dish, toss the peaches and blueberries with 6 tablespoons cubed butter, $\frac{1}{4}$ cup of the brown sugar, the maple syrup, and cornstarch. Bake until the blueberries are just beginning to burst, about 10 minutes. Remove from the oven, but leave the oven on.

3. Meanwhile, make the cinnamon spice sugar. In a small bowl, stir together the sugar, cinnamon, allspice, ginger, and a pinch of salt.

4. In a medium bowl, whisk together the flour, the remaining $\frac{3}{4}$ cup brown sugar, the baking powder, cinnamon, and salt. Add the sour cream, milk, and vanilla and mix until just combined. If your batter is super thick, stir in another splash or two of milk. Pour the batter over the baked peaches and blueberries; do not stir. Sprinkle the cinnamon sugar over the batter, then add the slices of cold butter.

5. Bake for 50 to 55 minutes, until the center is just set and the edges begin to brown. Serve the cobbler warm or at room temperature with ice cream.

note: To make your cobbler in mini skillets like mine, mix the peaches and blueberries with the cornstarch, $\frac{1}{4}$ cup of the brown sugar, the maple syrup, and melted butter. Divide the mixture among three 6-inch skillets. Bake for 10 minutes without the topping, then another 30 to 35 minutes after you add it.

classic tiramisu

PREP TIME 30 minutes · TOTAL TIME 30 minutes, plus chilling time · SERVES 6 to 8

I never thought I liked tiramisu, but the truth is . . . I only just recently tried it! Something about the coffee-soaked biscuits had me turning away. I don't know why—I love coffee! Regardless, it took me way too long to finally try tiramisu, and, of course, I fell in love with it. I first tried it at Bar Primi in New York. I was out to dinner with friends, and we ordered it for the table. It took only one bite, and I knew I needed to make my own recipe. After some experimenting, I think a great tiramisu needs to have a lot of cream and a heavy dusting of chocolate on top. The cream is my favorite part, so I double up on it. I even do a bit of whipped cream on top before serving. Then I give it a shower of chocolate curls, which are pretty and delicious, too! Make this a day or so ahead of time for the best flavor. That makes it great for dinner parties, plus it's easy!

16 ounces mascarpone, cold

4 large egg yolks, cold

1/2 cup heavy cream, cold

1/4 cup sugar

3 tablespoons dark rum

1 tablespoon pure vanilla extract

1/4 teaspoon ground ginger

1/4 teaspoon fine pink Himalayan salt

1 cup brewed espresso, cooled to room temperature

1/4 cup maple syrup

1 (7-ounce) package ladyfingers (24 cookies)

Unsweetened cocoa powder, for dusting

Whipped cream, for serving (optional)

Shaved chocolate, for serving

1. In a large bowl using an electric mixture, beat together the mascarpone, egg yolks, 1/4 cup of the heavy cream, the sugar, 1 tablespoon of the rum, the vanilla, ginger, and salt until combined and lightly whipped, about 2 minutes; do not overmix or the mascarpone will curdle.

2. In a separate medium bowl, whip the remaining 1/4 cup cream until soft peaks form. Using a rubber spatula, gently fold the whipped cream into the mascarpone cream.

3. In a shallow bowl, stir together the espresso, maple syrup, and remaining 2 tablespoons rum. Working with half of the ladyfingers, quickly dip one long side into the espresso mixture; do not let them sit in the liquid or they will get too soggy. Arrange the dipped ladyfingers in the bottom of a 9 x 9-inch baking dish, piecing them to fit as needed.

4. Spoon half of the mascarpone cream over the ladyfingers and dust generously with cocoa powder.

5. Dip the remaining ladyfingers in the espresso mixture, lining them up on top of the mascarpone cream as you work. Add the remaining cream over the top, spreading it in a smooth layer. Cover and chill for at least 4 hours or overnight.

6. Just before serving, top with whipped cream, if desired, then dust with more cocoa powder and garnish with chocolate shavings. Scoop and serve.

frosted peanut butter brownies

PREP TIME 20 minutes · COOK TIME 30 minutes · TOTAL TIME 50 minutes, plus cooling time · MAKES 16 brownies

I grew up in Ohio: the Buckeye State. If you live or have ever lived in Ohio, then you definitely know all about buckeyes—the dessert, not the things that grow on trees. Buckeyes are round balls of peanut butter covered in chocolate . . . basically a peanut butter cup, but in a different form. And they're delicious! It's impossible to eat just one. I love buckeyes, but you know what makes them even better? A brownie base. So that's exactly what I've done here! My crinkly fudge brownies get layered with sweetened peanut butter, then the sweetest chocolate frosting. These are just to die for. Make them during football season, especially when Ohio State is playing—these brownies will be the first snack to disappear.

1 cup (2 sticks) salted butter

2 cups semisweet chocolate chips

1½ cups granulated sugar

1 tablespoon pure vanilla extract

2 teaspoons instant coffee granules

4 large eggs, at room temperature

½ cup all-purpose flour

½ cup unsweetened cocoa powder

1 teaspoon baking powder

¾ cup creamy peanut butter, warmed

Frosting

4 tablespoons (½ stick) salted butter, at room temperature

2 cups powdered sugar

1 cup mini semisweet chocolate chips, melted (see Note)

½ cup milk of your choice, warmed

1 tablespoon creamy peanut butter

2 teaspoons pure vanilla extract

1. Preheat the oven to 350°F. Line a 9 x 9-inch baking dish with parchment paper, leaving a 1-inch overhang on two sides.

2. In a large microwave-safe bowl, combine the butter and 1½ cups of the chocolate chips. Microwave in 30-second intervals, stirring in between, until melted, about 2 minutes total. Stir in the sugar, vanilla, and instant coffee.

3. In a large bowl, vigorously whisk the eggs until bubbly on top, about 1 minute. Stir the eggs into the chocolate mixture. Add the flour, cocoa powder, and baking powder and stir until just combined. Stir in the remaining ½ cup chocolate chips. Transfer the batter to the prepared pan and spread evenly.

4. Bake until the brownies are just set in the center, 30 to 40 minutes. Remove from the oven and dollop spoonfuls of the warmed peanut butter over the top, lightly spreading it in an even layer. Let the brownies cool for about 30 minutes. Using the parchment overhang, remove the brownies from the baking dish.

5. Meanwhile, make the frosting. In a large bowl, combine the butter, powdered sugar, melted chocolate, ¼ cup of the warm milk, the peanut butter, and vanilla. Using an electric mixer, beat until smooth, 2 to 3 minutes, adding more milk as needed until the frosting is a spreadable consistency, but is still thin enough to spread easily.

6. Spread the frosting over the brownies. Let set for about an hour, then slice, snack, and enjoy! Store covered at room temperature for up to 5 days.

note: You can use regular chocolate chips if that's what you have handy, but I always like to use minis when melting because they do so more evenly.

browned butter coconut chocolate chip cookies

PREP TIME 15 minutes · **COOK TIME** 15 minutes · **TOTAL TIME** 30 minutes · **MAKES** about 24 cookies

These cookies are SO exciting to me. I actually think they are perfect. I have made them so many times, and they are now the most requested cookies from my family. Asher says that if I left out the coconut, they would be her favorite, but I LOVE the coconut. It's such an underrated baking ingredient, and when you pair it with nutty brown butter, the two flavors make magic. And then, the texture. They are my ideal, ever so slightly crisp on the edge, but soft, chewy, and gooey in the middle. The full two cups of chocolate chips make them heavy on the chocolate. Or if you're a real chocolate lover? Do half semisweet chocolate chips and half chopped chocolate chunks for bigger pockets of chocolate!

1 cup (2 sticks) salted butter

1 cup packed light or dark brown sugar

$1/4$ cup granulated sugar

2 large eggs

1 tablespoon pure vanilla extract

$1^1/4$ cups all-purpose flour

$1/2$ cup coconut flour

1 teaspoon baking soda

$1/2$ teaspoon fine pink Himalayan salt

$1^1/2$ cups chopped bittersweet chocolate chunks or chips

2 tablespoons sesame seeds

Flaky sea salt

1. Preheat the oven to 350°F. Line two baking sheets with parchment paper.

2. Place the butter in a small skillet over medium heat. Cook until the butter begins to brown, about 5 minutes. Transfer to a large heatproof bowl and set aside to cool for about 5 minutes, stirring occasionally.

3. To the brown butter, add the brown sugar, granulated sugar, eggs, and vanilla and stir until smooth. Add the all-purpose flour, coconut flour, baking soda, and pink salt and mix until just combined. If your dough feels too dry, stir in up to 2 tablespoons of water. Gently fold in the chocolate and sesame seeds, mixing just enough to combine.

4. Using 1 generously rounded tablespoon for each, roll the dough into balls. Arrange the balls on the prepared baking sheets, spacing them 2 inches apart. Gently press the dough down to slightly flatten.

5. Bake the cookies for 8 minutes. Remove the baking sheets from the oven and tap them firmly against the counter a few times to flatten the cookies. Return to the oven and bake until the cookies are just beginning to set on the edges, 2 to 3 minutes more.

6. Sprinkle the cookies with flaky salt and let them cool on the baking sheets; they will continue to cook slightly. Enjoy the cookies warm (highly recommended) or let cool and store at room temperature in an airtight container for up to 4 days.

raspberry white chocolate buttermilk cake

PREP TIME 30 minutes · COOK TIME 30 minutes · TOTAL TIME 1 hour, plus cooling time · SERVES 10

When I bake cakes, I usually go for a layer cake, but I can get excited about a sheet cake, too—especially since they take all the stress out of baking! This is my favorite fruit-based vanilla version. I use a combination of buttermilk, yogurt, and coconut oil, which results in the fluffiest cake with the best flavor that's heavy on the vanilla in the most delicious way. I make this a lot in the summer when berries are plentiful at the market. I will often swap the raspberries for blueberries or strawberries, depending on what looks best. Be sure to use a high-quality raspberry jam—homemade or from a local farm stand is always best, but Bonne Maman is my go-to brand from the store.

1 cup melted coconut oil, plus more for greasing

½ cup plain Greek yogurt or sour cream

3 large eggs, at room temperature

1 cup granulated sugar

1½ cups buttermilk

1 tablespoon pure vanilla extract

3¾ cups all-purpose flour

2 teaspoons baking powder

1 teaspoon baking soda

1 teaspoon fine pink Himalayan salt

4 ounces chopped white chocolate or white chocolate chips

1½ cups raspberry preserves or jam (I like Bonne Maman)

Zest and juice of 1 lemon

Fresh raspberries, for decorating

White Chocolate Frosting

8 ounces white chocolate

1½ cups (3 sticks) salted butter, at room temperature

1½ cups powdered sugar

2 teaspoons pure vanilla extract

1. Preheat the oven to 350°F. Coat the insides of a 9 x 13-inch baking dish with coconut oil.

2. In a large bowl, beat together the coconut oil, yogurt, eggs, sugar, buttermilk, and vanilla. Add the flour, baking powder, baking soda, and salt and mix until just combined. Fold in the chopped white chocolate.

3. Transfer the batter to the prepared pan. Using about half of the preserves, dollop spoonfuls over the cake. Use a knife to gently swirl the preserves into the batter; do not overmix.

4. Bake until a tester inserted into the center comes out clean, 30 to 35 minutes. Remove from the oven and let cool completely, about 30 minutes.

5. Meanwhile, make the frosting. In a microwave-safe bowl, microwave the white chocolate in 30-second intervals, stirring in between, until melted. Let cool.

6. In a large bowl, use an electric mixer to beat together the butter and powdered sugar until light and fluffy, scraping down the sides as needed, 3 to 4 minutes. Add the melted white chocolate and vanilla and beat until combined, about 1 minute more.

7. In a small bowl, stir together the remaining preserves with the lemon zest and juice. Reserving a small amount to finish the cake, spread a thin layer of frosting over the cake, then frost the cake all over. Add small spoonfuls of the reserved fruit mixture to the frosting and gently swirl. Top with raspberries, then slice and serve. Store covered at room temperature for up to 5 days.

maple banana pudding

PREP TIME 15 minutes · **COOK TIME** 10 minutes · **TOTAL TIME** 25 minutes, plus chilling time · **SERVES** 6 to 8

I like a banana pudding that's pretty classic: creamy, rich, and packed with vanilla flavor. It must have the OG vanilla wafer cookies, too, because there is nothing better than those, especially when it comes to this dessert. I make my pudding very simply, but the secret ingredient to note is the vanilla bean powder. It's a little pricey, but it really adds the most rich and delicious flavor. I love to use vanilla bean powder when I'm making any kind of pudding or ice cream, so I always keep a jar in the pantry. If you want to add an extra special finish, try dusting the top of the bananas with cinnamon. If you prefer to not use dairy, coconut milk is a wonderful, delicious substitution for both the whole milk and the heavy cream. It will add a subtle, sweet coconut flavor, which tastes great here.

2 cups whole milk

$1/4$ cup cornstarch

2 cups heavy cream

$1/2$ cup maple syrup

1 teaspoon vanilla bean powder (optional)

$1/2$ teaspoon fine pink Himalayan salt

1 tablespoon pure vanilla extract

30 vanilla wafer cookies, gently crushed

4 ripe but firm bananas, sliced

1. In a large pan, whisk together $1/2$ cup of the milk and the cornstarch. Whisk in the remaining $1^1/2$ cups milk, 1 cup of the heavy cream, the maple syrup, vanilla bean powder (if using), and salt. Set the pan over medium-high heat and bring to a boil. Cook, stirring constantly, until the mixture thickens and becomes creamy and pudding-like, about 5 minutes, adjusting the heat as needed to keep it from scorching. Remove the pan from the heat and stir in the vanilla extract.

2. Strain the mixture through a fine-mesh sieve set over a large bowl. Let cool for 5 minutes, then cover with plastic wrap, placing the wrap directly on the surface of the mixture. Cool completely in the fridge, at least 2 hours.

3. In a medium bowl, use an electric mixer to beat the remaining 1 cup cream until stiff peaks form. Working in batches, fold the whipped cream into the pudding.

4. To assemble, in the bottom of 6 to 8 glass jars or cups, layer the crushed cookies, sliced bananas, and pudding. Repeat each layer once more. Chill in the refrigerator for at least 30 minutes or up to overnight. Serve topped with more crushed cookies.

note: Alternatively, you can assemble the pudding in a large trifle bowl, following the same pattern.

blackout sprinkle cookies

PREP TIME 20 minutes · **COOK TIME** 10 minutes
TOTAL TIME 30 minutes, plus cooling time · **MAKES** about 42 cookies

How cute are these cookies? They almost remind me of a chocolate glazed doughnut. One of the best things about these cookies, at least in my opinion, is that you can choose how you want to make the icing: with either avocado oil or milk. If you use milk, you get a really creamy, dark, and rich glaze that stays softer on the cookies. It's delicious and leaves you with chocolaty fingers—fun! With the oil, you'll get a stiffer glaze that hardens as it sets. Both are equally delicious—it's more of a texture thing. Pick your poison . . . or be like me and make BOTH! Obviously, the sprinkles at the end make these even sweeter!

1 cup (2 sticks) salted butter, at room temperature

1 cup sugar

2 teaspoons pure vanilla extract

1 large egg

1¾ cups all-purpose flour

½ cup unsweetened cocoa powder

1 teaspoon baking soda

½ teaspoon fine pink Himalayan salt

⅓ cup mini semisweet chocolate chips

Glaze

1 cup mini semisweet chocolate chips (see Note, page 252)

2 tablespoons avocado oil or ⅓ cup milk of your choice

Chocolate sprinkles, for decorating

Crushed, freeze-dried strawberries or raspberries, for decorating

1. Preheat the oven to 350°F. Line two baking sheets with parchment paper.

2. In a large bowl, use an electric mixer to beat together the butter, sugar, and vanilla until smooth and fluffy, scraping down the sides as needed, about 4 minutes. Add the egg and continue beating until fully combined, about 1 minute. Add the flour, cocoa powder, baking soda, and salt and beat on low just enough to combine, about 1 minute more. Stir in the chocolate chips.

3. Using 1 tablespoon for each, roll the dough into balls. Arrange them on the prepared baking sheets, spacing them 2 inches apart.

4. Bake the cookies for 5 minutes. Rotate the baking sheets and continue baking for another 5 to 6 minutes or until the cookies are just beginning to set on the edges. Remove from the oven and let cool on the baking sheets; they will continue to cook slightly.

5. Meanwhile, make the glaze. In a small microwave-safe bowl, microwave the chocolate chips and oil together in 30-second intervals, stirring after each, until completely melted and smooth.

6. Dip each cookie in the glaze. Decorate as desired with sprinkles and/or crushed strawberries. Let set or serve immediately. Store in an airtight container at room temperature for up to 5 days.

salty caramel rice crisp treats

PREP TIME 10 minutes · **COOK TIME** 15 minutes
TOTAL TIME 25 minutes, plus cooling time · **MAKES** 24 squares

I rarely make Rice Krispie Treats, but when I do, I make this version because I think they are superior to a basic back-of-the-box version. The brown butter swirled through these chewy, sweet, and crunchy bars is just magic. Not everyone realizes what it is, but they do taste the nutty, toasty, vanilla-like flavor it adds. It is a game changer. If you make these treats for a bake sale, you'll totally steal the show.

1 cup (2 sticks) salted butter, plus more for greasing

½ cup packed dark brown sugar

½ cup heavy cream

1 teaspoon fine pink Himalayan salt

2 (10-ounce) bags mini marshmallows

8 cups rice crisp cereal (I like Barbara's or Whole Foods 365 brown rice crisps)

Flaky sea salt

1. Grease a 9 x 13-inch baking dish.

2. In a large pot over medium heat, melt the butter. Continue to cook, stirring often, until the butter begins to brown and smells lightly toasted, 5 to 6 minutes. Remove from the heat and let the butter cool for about 5 minutes.

3. Using a rubber spatula, stir the brown sugar and cream into the butter. Return to medium heat, bring to a gentle boil, and cook, stirring constantly, until the sugar has melted and the mixture is dark and bubbling, about 5 minutes. Stir in the fine salt. Add the marshmallows and stir vigorously until fully melted, about 5 minutes. Remove from the heat.

4. Add the cereal and stir to mix well and coat evenly. Immediately transfer the mixture to the prepared pan, working quickly to spread it evenly and packing it in tightly. Sprinkle with flaky salt.

5. Let cool for at least 1 hour. Cut into bars and serve. Store at room temperature in an airtight container for up to 5 days.

dark chocolate pistachio cake
with cream cheese icing

PREP TIME 20 minutes · **COOK TIME** 1 hour · **TOTAL TIME** 1 hour 20 minutes, plus cooling and setting time · **SERVES** 8 to 10

I think pistachios are overlooked as a super delicious ingredient. They are mostly seen in rich desserts, like baklava, or used on a cheese board. Those are yummy, but I love to bake them into many sweet treats—and I adore this pistachio cake. Grinding the pistachios into a flour creates the tastiest cake, and the honey is not only the perfect sweetener but it also highlights the salty flavors. I usually add a cream cheese icing, but the cake is great all on its own, too! I bake this over the holidays into mini loaves, then package them up and use them as host/hostess gifts for friends and family. If you're baking this cake in the summer, try adding raspberries!

1 cup shelled roasted pistachios, plus more for serving

1 cup white whole-wheat pastry flour or all-purpose flour

2 teaspoons baking powder

1/2 teaspoon fine pink Himalayan salt

1 cup sour cream or plain Greek yogurt

1/2 cup honey

1/2 cup extra-virgin olive oil

3 large eggs

1 tablespoon pure vanilla extract

1 tablespoon orange zest

1 cup chopped dark chocolate, plus more for serving

Dried rose petals, for serving

Cream Cheese Icing

3 cups powdered sugar

1/4 cup milk of your choice, warmed, plus more as needed

2 ounces cream cheese, at room temperature

2 teaspoons pure vanilla extract

1. Preheat the oven to 350°F. Line a 9 x 5-inch loaf pan with parchment paper, leaving a 1-inch overhang on each short side.

2. In a blender or food processor, pulse the pistachios until very finely ground to the consistency of flour, 1 to 2 minutes. Transfer to a large bowl.

3. Add the flour, baking powder, and salt to the ground pistachios and whisk to combine. Add the sour cream, honey, olive oil, eggs, vanilla, and orange zest and stir until well combined. Fold in the chopped chocolate. Transfer the batter to the prepared pan and use a spatula to smooth the top.

4. Bake until the center is just set, 50 to 60 minutes. Remove from the oven and let cool for about 30 minutes.

5. Meanwhile, make the cream cheese icing. In a medium bowl, stir together the powdered sugar, milk, cream cheese, and vanilla, adding more milk as needed to reach a pourable consistency.

6. Use the overhang to remove the loaf from the pan and transfer it to a wire rack. Pour the icing over the loaf and top with more chocolate, pistachios, and/or rose petals, if desired. Let set for about 1 hour or enjoy immediately. Store covered in the fridge for up to 5 days.

cashew coffee milkshake

PREP TIME 10 minutes · **TOTAL TIME** 10 minutes · **SERVES** 1

I hesitated to call this a milkshake, since it doesn't have any ice cream in it—but even still, it's just as creamy and just as yummy! This reminds me of the vanilla milkshakes my dad would make us when we were growing up. A mix of milk (I recommend whole milk here), cashew butter, and hemp seed creates the creamiest base, and don't forget to add the vanilla. The dates sweeten it up wonderfully, and the coffee provides a little something extra (deliciousness!). Of course, you can leave it out if you prefer, and feel free to add your favorite protein powder.

1 cup milk of your choice

4 to 6 pitted medjool dates

⅓ cup plain Greek yogurt

1 to 2 shots brewed espresso, cooled to room temperature

1 tablespoon cashew butter

1 tablespoon hemp seeds (optional)

2 teaspoons pure vanilla extract

Fine pink Himalayan salt

Espresso powder, for serving

1. In a blender, combine the milk and dates and let sit until the dates are softened, about 10 minutes. Add the yogurt, espresso, cashew butter, hemp seeds (if using), vanilla, a pinch of salt, and a big handful of ice. Blend on high until smooth and frothy, about 3 minutes.

2. Pour into a glass and top with espresso powder to finish. Enjoy!

baked blackberry lavender doughnuts

PREP TIME 15 minutes · **COOK TIME** 15 minutes · **TOTAL TIME** 30 minutes · **MAKES** 6 doughnuts

In the summertime, one of my favorite flavor combinations is blackberry and lavender. I have a three-layer cake on the website that has been crowd-pleaser for years and years now. It's a showstopper and totally delish! These doughnuts have those same sweet flavors and beautiful colors, but they're so much faster to make. Plus, doughnuts are always a surprising, fun treat. Feel free to use your favorite berries in place of the blackberries—blueberries or strawberries would be great here!

4 tablespoons ($\frac{1}{2}$ stick) salted butter, melted, plus more for greasing

$\frac{3}{4}$ cup milk of your choice, plus more as needed

1 tablespoon dried culinary lavender

2 large eggs, at room temperature

$\frac{1}{2}$ cup maple syrup

$\frac{1}{4}$ cup blackberry preserves or jam (I like Bonne Maman)

1 tablespoon pure vanilla extract

2 cups white whole-wheat or all-purpose flour

$1\frac{1}{2}$ teaspoons baking powder

$\frac{1}{2}$ teaspoon fine pink Himalayan salt

$\frac{1}{3}$ cup chopped blackberries

$1\frac{1}{2}$ cups powdered sugar, plus more as needed

1. Preheat the oven to 350°F. Grease a 6-cup doughnut tin.

2. In a small saucepan, combine the milk and lavender. Place over medium heat and bring to a gentle boil, then simmer, stirring, for 2 minutes. Remove from the heat, cover, and let steep for 10 minutes, until fragrant and infused. Strain out and discard the lavender.

3. In a large bowl, whisk together $\frac{1}{2}$ cup of the steeped lavender milk, the melted butter, eggs, maple syrup, preserves, and vanilla. Add the flour, baking powder, and salt and stir until just combined. Gently fold in the berries. Divide the batter evenly among the doughnut cups, filling each half to two-thirds of the way.

4. Bake until the doughnuts are just set, about 12 minutes. Remove from the oven and let cool in the pan for 5 minutes, then run a knife around the edges to release and invert the pan.

5. Meanwhile, make the glaze. Transfer the remaining $\frac{1}{4}$ cup steeped lavender milk to a medium bowl. Whisk in the powdered sugar, adding more sugar or milk as needed to achieve a consistency that's pourable but not runny.

6. Dip the doughnuts into the glaze or drizzle it over the tops. Serve immediately or store at room temperature in an airtight container for up to 5 days.

old-fashioned chocolate sheet cake

PREP TIME 25 minutes · **COOK TIME** 30 minutes · **TOTAL TIME** 55 minutes, plus cooling and setting time · **SERVES** 8 to 10

Whenever I'm craving a rich and delicious chocolate cake (or my mom or sister is), I make this one. It's sooo fluffy and moist. I love really going for it with the vanilla to give it a delicious flavor. The frosting is fun, too. It's more in the style of that old-school sort of icing that your grandma might have frosted her cakes with. You pour the frosting over the top of the cake, then let it set up. Nothing fancy! Top it with chocolate shavings and sprinkles.

1 cup melted coconut oil, plus more for greasing

1½ cups all-purpose flour

1½ cups granulated sugar

1 cup unsweetened cocoa powder

1 teaspoon baking soda

1 teaspoon fine pink Himalayan salt

1 cup hot brewed coffee

1 tablespoon pure vanilla extract

2 large eggs

1 cup milk of your choice

½ cup mini semisweet chocolate chips

Chocolate shavings or sprinkles, for decorating

Frosting

½ cup (1 stick) salted butter, melted

2½ cups powdered sugar, plus more as needed

½ cup unsweetened cocoa powder

⅓ cup milk of your choice, warm, plus more as needed

1 tablespoon pure vanilla extract

1. Preheat the oven to 350°F. Grease a 9 x 13-inch baking dish with coconut oil.

2. In a large bowl, stir together the flour, sugar, cocoa powder, baking soda, and salt. In a medium bowl, whisk together the coconut oil, coffee, and vanilla. Pour the coconut oil mixture into the flour mixture, then add the eggs and milk. Using a rubber spatula, mix until just combined; the batter will be thin. Pour the batter into the prepared pan and sprinkle chocolate chips over the top.

3. Bake until the top is just set, the cake is no longer wiggly in the center, and a toothpick inserted in the center comes out clean, 30 to 35 minutes. Remove from the oven and let cool for about 30 minutes.

4. Meanwhile, make the frosting. In a large bowl, use an electric mixer to mix together the butter, powdered sugar, cocoa powder, warm milk, and vanilla until smooth, adding additional warm milk as needed until the frosting becomes thicker, but still drizzly, about 1 minute. Taste and mix in more powdered sugar as needed to reach your desired sweetness.

5. Working quickly, immediately spread the frosting over the cake. Let set for about 1 hour. Top with chocolate shavings, then slice and serve. Store covered at room temperature for up to 5 days.

chewy pumpkin cookies
with maple icing

PREP TIME 30 minutes · COOK TIME 15 minutes · TOTAL TIME 45 minutes · MAKES 24 cookies

Pumpkin cookies can be tricky. I find they are often a bit too cakey and never have enough pumpkin flavor. I have tried so many recipes, but I've just never loved a pumpkin cookie . . . until now! The key is to use pumpkin butter instead of canned pumpkin puree. It's much more concentrated and creamier than the puree, and it has THE most delicious pumpkin flavor. It's what makes these cookies so special. They have the most perfect chewy edge with very soft (but not cakey!) centers, plus puddles of melted chocolate chunks. I'm obsessed. These will be everyone's favorite autumn cookies, and if you make these for Thanksgiving, they'll be the first dessert to disappear. Tip: Always make a double batch!

1 cup (2 sticks) salted butter

1 cup packed light or dark brown sugar

$1/3$ cup pumpkin butter

$1/4$ cup maple syrup

1 large egg

2 teaspoons pure vanilla extract

$2^1/3$ cups all-purpose flour, plus more as needed

$1^1/2$ teaspoons pumpkin pie spice, or 1 teaspoon ground cinnamon

1 teaspoon baking soda

$1/2$ teaspoon fine pink Himalayan salt

$1^1/2$ cups semisweet chocolate chunks

Flaky sea salt (optional)

Maple Icing

$1/2$ cup (1 stick) salted butter

$1^1/2$ cups powdered sugar

$1/3$ cup maple syrup

Fine pink Himalayan salt

1. Preheat the oven to 350°F. Line two baking sheets with parchment paper.

2. In a small skillet over medium heat, melt the butter. Continue cooking until the butter begins to brown, about 5 minutes. Transfer to a large heatproof bowl and set aside to cool for about 5 minutes.

3. To the brown butter, add the brown sugar, pumpkin butter, maple syrup, egg, and vanilla and stir until smooth. Add the flour, pumpkin pie spice, baking soda, and pink salt and mix to combine well. Stir in the chocolate chunks.

4. Using 1 generously rounded tablespoon for each, roll the dough into balls. It might be a little bit sticky; if so, lightly flour your hands. Arrange the balls on the prepared baking sheets, spacing them 2 inches apart. Gently press the dough down to slightly flatten.

5. Bake the cookies for 8 minutes. Remove the baking sheets from the oven and tap them firmly against the counter a few times to flatten the cookies. Return to the oven and bake until the cookies are just beginning to set on the edges, 2 to 3 minutes more. Let the cookies cool on the baking sheets; they will continue to cook slightly.

6. While the cookies cool, make the maple icing. In a small skillet over medium heat, melt the butter. Continue to cook until the butter begins to brown and smells toasted, about 5 minutes. Remove from the heat and whisk in the powdered sugar, maple syrup, and a pinch of salt.

7. The icing sets quickly, so work fast and immediately spread it over the cookies. Sprinkle with flaky salt, if you like. Serve immediately, or let cool and store at room temperature in an airtight container for up to 5 days.

apple honey cake

PREP TIME 20 minutes · **COOK TIME** 1 hour 5 minutes · **TOTAL TIME** 1 hour 25 minutes · **SERVES** 8

This is the coziest autumn cake. I start making it at the beginning of September, as soon as apples are back in season. My secret is using a rich, sweet, spiced apple butter. It adds so much flavor and moisture to the cake. Be sure to cut your apples super thin—I think the texture of the cake is best that way. Oh, and the ginger cinnamon sugar will shock you (in a good way!). The chewy candied ginger mixed in is delicious. Serve this warm with lots of honey butter.

$1\frac{1}{2}$ cups apple cider

4 tablespoons ($\frac{1}{2}$ stick) salted butter

2 large eggs

$\frac{1}{2}$ cup Maple Apple Butter (page 195) or store-bought apple butter

$\frac{1}{2}$ cup honey

1 tablespoon pure vanilla extract

2 cups white whole-wheat or all-purpose flour

1 rounded tablespoon apple pie or pumpkin pie spice

$1\frac{1}{2}$ teaspoons baking soda

1 teaspoon ground cinnamon

$\frac{1}{2}$ teaspoon fine pink Himalayan salt

2 cups very thinly sliced Honeycrisp apples (from 2 to 3 apples)

Ginger Cinnamon Sugar

$\frac{1}{4}$ cup crystallized ginger, roughly chopped

$\frac{1}{2}$ cup sugar

2 tablespoons cold salted butter

1 teaspoon ground cinnamon

Honey Butter (optional)

4 tablespoons ($\frac{1}{2}$ stick) salted butter, at room temperature

$\frac{1}{4}$ cup honey

Pinch of fine pink Himalayan salt

1. Preheat the oven to 350°F. Line a 9 x 9-inch baking dish with parchment paper, leaving a 1-inch overhang on two sides.

2. In a small pan, bring the apple cider to a boil over high heat. Reduce the heat to low and simmer until reduced to $\frac{1}{2}$ cup, about 20 minutes. Remove from the heat and stir in the butter to melt. Let cool for 5 minutes.

3. Pour the reduced cider mixture into a large bowl. Add the eggs, apple butter, honey, and vanilla and stir to combine. Add the flour, apple pie spice, baking soda, cinnamon, and salt. Stir until just combined. Fold in the apples; it will feel like too many apples and that's okay. Spoon the batter evenly into the prepared pan.

4. Make the ginger cinnamon sugar. In a blender or food processor, pulse the ginger until a paste forms, about 30 seconds. Add the sugar, butter, and cinnamon and pulse to combine. Sprinkle the sugar mixture evenly over the cake.

5. Bake until the center of the cake is just set, 45 to 55 minutes. Remove from the oven and let cool for 5 minutes. Using the parchment overhang as handles, remove the cake from the baking dish.

6. Meanwhile, if desired, make the honey butter. In a small bowl, combine the butter, honey, and salt.

7. Slice the cake and serve warm, slathered with the honey butter, if desired. Store covered at room temperature for up to 5 days.

carrot cake cupcakes
with cream cheese frosting

PREP TIME 25 minutes · COOK TIME 20 minutes · TOTAL TIME 45 minutes, plus cooling time · MAKES 12 cupcakes

I can think of exactly two people in my life who love carrot cake. These two ladies were eating a big slice of it the first time I met them at Monkey Bar in New York City. Now when I bake any kind of carrot cake, I think of them. And I made sure they gave these cupcakes their seal of approval because they are, after all, my carrot cake girls. Of course, we all know they just had to have frosting, too. Carrot cake just isn't complete without it! I like to add micro mums for an extra-pretty finish—they're edible flowers that you can find online.

Cupcakes

$1/2$ cup melted coconut oil

$1/2$ cup maple syrup

2 large eggs

1 tablespoon pure vanilla extract

$1 1/2$ cups grated carrots

$1 1/2$ cups white whole-wheat pastry flour

1 teaspoon plus 1 tablespoon ground cinnamon

$1 1/2$ teaspoons baking powder

$1/2$ teaspoon baking soda

$1/2$ teaspoon ground cardamom

$1/2$ teaspoon ground ginger

$1/2$ teaspoon fine pink Himalayan salt

$1/4$ teaspoon freshly grated nutmeg

$1/4$ cup granulated sugar

Frosting

2 ounces cream cheese, at room temperature

2 tablespoons salted butter, at room temperature

$1/4$ cup powdered sugar

1 tablespoon milk of choice, plus more as needed

2 teaspoons pure vanilla extract

1. **Make the cupcakes.** Preheat the oven to 350°F. Line a 12-cup muffin tin with paper liners.

2. In a large bowl, whisk together the coconut oil, maple syrup, eggs, and vanilla. Stir in the carrots. Add the flour, 1 teaspoon cinnamon, the baking powder, baking soda, cardamom, ginger, salt, and nutmeg. Stir until just combined. In a small bowl, stir together the granulated sugar and the remaining 1 tablespoon cinnamon.

3. Divide the batter among the prepared muffin cups. Evenly sprinkle the cinnamon sugar over each cupcake. Bake until they are just set and a tester inserted into the center of a cupcake comes out clean, 18 to 20 minutes.

4. **Meanwhile, make the frosting.** In a medium bowl, use an electric mixer on medium speed to beat together the cream cheese and butter just until smooth Add the powdered sugar, milk, and vanilla. Beat until mixed well, adding more milk if needed, one teaspoon at a time, to reach a thin, runny consistency.

5. Let the cupcakes cool in the pan for about 5 minutes, then remove and let cool on a wire rack for another 5 minutes. While they're still warm, drizzle the cupcakes with frosting, making sure it drips into every nook and cranny. Serve warm or at room temperature. Store in an airtight container at room temperature for up to 5 days.

acknowledgments

This book would not be here today without the incredible team that helped me make it. It has truly been a group effort, and I feel so lucky to work with the people I get to work with. They are the most supportive and want nothing more than to see me succeed and to create an amazing cookbook together!

To Amanda Englander, without whom this cookbook literally would not exist today. Thank you for putting in the hours, working with me at 11:00 p.m. New York time, dealing with my craziness, and always having my back. This is our fourth book together, and I truly think it is our best. Thank you to the moon and back.

To Francis Lam, I really put you through it with this book, but you stuck with me through the entire process. While there may have been a fear of not getting this done, you never doubted my willpower. I can't express my gratitude for your part in making this book come to life.

To the rest of the team at Clarkson Potter—Terry Deal, Stephanie Huntwork, Jan Derevjanik, Kim Tyner, Christina Self, Neil Spitkovsky, Alex Noya, Raquel Pelzel, Darian Keels, Derek Gullino, Kate Tyler, Kristin Casemore, and Stephanie Davis—you all really came through for me, and I appreciate your hard work more than you know! I know this book was not the easiest one we've worked on together, but I think we are all so excited by how it turned out!

To Ashleigh Amoroso, you jumped in and took charge. I can't even begin to express my gratitude. You were an open ear to vent to, you created the most beautiful sets for me, and you moved mountains to help me cross the finish line. I am so lucky to have met you and now call you a good friend. Your talent and kindness will never go unnoticed. Thank you!

To Kristen Kilpatrick, the one and only. You will literally do anything and everything for me, and you have been here through it all—this is now our fourth book together! You are the most talented photographer, and I love you for understanding how to make me look the cutest. Thank you for being the best friend that you are and for meeting insane deadlines just because I needed you to. You are an angel.

To Fatima Khawaja and Ben Weiner, thank you for cooking through every single one of these recipes, and even more that didn't make the cut. Your patience and diligence are so appreciated!

To Andy Barzvi, thank you for putting up with me and always sticking your neck out for me. I am lucky to have such a wonderful person like you always coming to bat for me. You are the best of the best in the literary world.

To my wonderful HBH team, you girls put up with a lot and always keep me on track. Thank you for always being the most supportive and never letting anything slip through the cracks. I love you!

To my siblings, for constantly inspiring me and entertaining me—especially Asher for being the best sister a girl could ask for, and Creighton for being a total pro at taste testing.

To my dad, who none of this could happen without—thank you for the grocery shopping, cleaning, and therapy sessions. And, of course, to my mom, to whom I really owe everything. She runs the show, and without her nothing would happen. Thank you for always being there for me!

There are countless other people I wish I could mention and show my love for, but we would be here for days. Thank you to everyone who touched this book and has supported me along the way!

index

Note: Page references in italics indicate photographs.

CLARKSON POTTER is a trademark and
POTTER with colophon is a registered trademark
of Penguin Random House LLC.

Library of Congress Cataloging-in-Publication
Data is on file with the publisher.

ISBN 978-0-593-23257-6
Ebook ISBN 978-0-593-23258-3

Printed in China

Contributing editor: Amanda Englander
Editor: Francis Lam
Editorial assistant: Darian Keels
Designer: Jan Derevjanik
Art director: Stephanie Huntwork
Lifestyle photographer: Kristen Kilpatrick
Production editor: Terry Deal
Production editorial assistants: Taylor Teague
and Leni Schenkel
Production manager: Kim Tyner
Production designer: Christina Self
Compositor: Merri Ann Morrell
Copy editor: Pat Dailey
Proofreaders: Rachel Holzman,
Mark McCauslin, and Sigi Nacson
Indexer: Elizabeth T. Parson
Publicists: Kate Tyler and Kristin Casemore
Marketer: Stephanie Davis

10 9 8 7 6 5 4 3 2 1

First Edition